THE FIVE AND A HALF QUESTIONS EVERYONE MUST ANSWER

In Search of Purposeful Identity

JOE PELLEGRINO

with
CRAIG LIVSEY

Contents

This book is dedicated to my awesome family, as well as my good friend, Craig Livsey, who provided so much help in giving this book life! But most of all I want to give praise to my Lord and Savior Jesus Christ who took a deeply self-centered man and miraculously transformed him! Finally, I would also like to give a shout out to all those "Average Joe's" who are about to discover the power that lies within!

Before you start we recommend that you download the PDF of the Tools that we discuss in this book. To do so please visit NotJustanAverageJoe.com/Tools

Introduction

There's a terrifying journey, which everyone must take:
the expedition of one's heart to tend that subtle ache.
But the hollow of the heart is strange and cavernous,
filled with crystal wonders and dank labyrinths.
There are treasures to unearth, and looters know this well.
Take heed and haste to find where yours may dwell.
— JENNIFER PELLEGRINO

THE SILENT KILLER

A silent killer exists in our homes, our workplaces, our churches, and our communities. This killer doesn't use violence to claim its victims, but he can destroy and even take lives. If this killer goes unnoticed, he has the power to rip apart the very fabric of our society.

This killer is the Identity Thief (Satan), and his sole purpose is to make you believe you're something you're not. He deceives you into believing lies and then tells you to pour those same lies into others.

The Five and a Half Questions Everyone Must Answer addresses this killer. It will help you better understand your true identity and, from there, point you to the purpose for which you were created. To do this, you'll need to be honest with yourself and ask others to be truthful with you as well. In the process, you may uncover some things you won't want to hear, but addressing these things is necessary to get you where you need to go.

WHO AM I?

I hope the first section made you sit up and take notice, but if I were you, I would want to know who is dispensing this advice. So let's start with a little bit about me. I had good people for parents, people whom others liked—good people but not great teachers. In our home, there was no encouragement, nurturing, or discipline, at least for me. Dissatisfied with who I was, and truthfully unaware of who I could be, I created my own little world, a world where I was somebody. This led to the telling of many lies that supported my brave, new fantasy world —so many lies that, to this day, I'm not sure what was real about my childhood.

You see, when we keep telling ourselves lies, it blurs our sense of reality, and my reality was obscure! My entire identity, merely fantasy, didn't do me any good. I became a thief, a cheat, and a scam artist focused only on myself—the perfect narcissist. As a result, I made mistakes—*big* mistakes—and bridges burned. Then everything changed for me on Saturday, May 27, 1995. On that day, my eyes were open to who I *should* be, my true identity. (More about this later.)

As a result, I began making some real changes in my life, wanting to build something substantial, something real. A powerful life that would impact generations to come. The road wasn't easy, but it was one I had to travel to meet my true self—the man I was created to be —and to walk in my God-given calling.

During this time, I experienced two great hardships. They brought me face-to-face with who I was. They put the "new" Joe to the test. The first was losing a company, the other a damaging flood. While extremely painful and challenging, these two valley experiences were the catalyst—in my opinion, God's roadmap—to get me where I needed to be, the *real* me. I recognized and embraced that truth. (More about these hardships later.)

Like all of us, I've had highs and lows. At the end of the day, I know I'm just an average Joe—a regular, unspectacular man. But I believe the Bible teaches that if we truly know Jesus as our Lord and Savior, there is greatness in us. Greatness that most of us put a cap on, never to be released. Let's face it: the cemeteries are filled with millions of books never written, serums never invented, music never composed, and truths that were never shared. But I was determined to find and release this power within me—this greatness—not for my glory but for the one who rescued me.

So how can you not end up like one of those who take their unexercised gifts to the grave? That's why I've put together this book. You see, along the way, I found 5.5 questions that needed—no, *demanded*—an answer before I could unlock that power within. These simple yet impactful questions changed the way I looked at my life and allowed me to see myself through the eyes of others. Now I know that these 5.5 questions are the very same questions that everyone *must* answer.

If you're ready, let's get started.

THE OBJECTIVE

This book is designed to help you take an introspective journey into discovering

- how you are *really* wired,
- what *really* drives you,
- what's *really* important to you in life, and
- why you were *really* created.

In other words, your *real* purposeful identity. And it all starts with one extreme, courageous question: Who are you ... *really*?

WHO ARE YOU REALLY?

Let's be honest. We all have struggles. Yes, *all* of us.

Take Horatio G. Spafford as an example. A successful lawyer in the Chicago area during the late-1800s, he experienced tremendous loss and devastation. At the age of two, his son died of pneumonia. Then in 1871, the Great Chicago fire ruined him financially, as many of his investments had been in Chicago property. But the greatest tragedy he and his wife would experience happened just two years later, in 1873, with the economic downturn.

Managing this tragedy kept Spafford in Chicago while the rest of his family (his wife and four daughters) went off on their planned trip to Europe via the *SS Ville du Havre*. While crossing the Atlantic Ocean, the *Ville du Havre* collided with a three-masted Scottish sea vessel, the *Loch Earn*. Spafford's wife, Anna, hurriedly gathered her four daughters on deck and prayed that if it was God's will, he would spare their lives. Anna was later found floating on some wreckage from the *Ville du Havre*, but their four daughters, along with 226 other passengers and crew members, were lost. After being rescued nine days later, Anna arrived in Cardiff, Wales, where she wired her husband a simple, devastating telegram: "Saved alone, what shall I do?"

Immediately, Spafford booked passage to meet his grieving wife. Four days into their journey, the captain called him into his cabin to tell him that they were over the general place where his daughters had drowned. The grave reality of his daughters' deaths, added to the significant trials he was already suffering, compelled him to pen these words:

When peace, like a river, attendeth my way,
When sorrows like sea billows roll;
Whatever my lot, Thou hast taught me to say,
It is well; it is well with my soul.

Refrain:

It is well with my soul,
It is well; it is well with my soul.
Though Satan should buffet, though trials should come,
Let this blest assurance control,
That Christ hath regarded my helpless estate,
And hath shed His own blood for my soul.

My sin—oh, the bliss of this glorious thought! —
My sin, not in part but the whole,
Is nailed to the cross, and I bear it no more,
Praise the Lord, praise the Lord, O my soul!

For me, be it Christ, be it Christ hence to live:
If Jordan above me shall roll,
No pang shall be mine, for in death as in life,
Thou wilt whisper Thy peace to my soul.

But, Lord, 'tis for Thee, for Thy coming we wait,
The sky, not the grave, is our goal;
Oh, trump of the angel! Oh, voice of the Lord!
Blessed hope, blessed rest of my soul!

And Lord, haste the day when the faith shall be sight,
The clouds be rolled back as a scroll;
The trump shall resound, and the Lord shall descend,
Even so, it is well with my soul.

These are the words of the well-known hymn "It Is Well with My Soul," an incredible testament to Spafford's unwavering faith in the goodness of God no matter the struggles he allows. Spafford's faith was active. Writing "Whatever my lot, thou hast taught me to say, / It is well, it is well with my soul" was no doubt painfully poignant as he encountered his daughters' burial ground. Yet, in faith, he still declared the goodness of God. He took an active step forward.

Anna gave birth to three more children after this. One would die at the age of four, another victim of pneumonia. Their church regarded their ongoing tragedy as divine punishment, but Spafford knew this was a lie. He heeded God's call and moved his family to Jerusalem, where they settled for the rest of his life. There the family formed their sect and founded a group called the American Colony, which engaged in philanthropic work and gained the trust of Muslims, Jews, and Christians alike.

Imagine if Spafford had allowed his struggles and hardships to define him or overwhelm him. Imagine if he had allowed "sorrows like sea billows" to swallow him. But it was one truth alone that fortified him: "My sin, oh the bliss of this glorious thought! / My sin, not in part but the whole, / is nailed to the cross, and I bear it no more, / Praise the Lord, praise the Lord, O my soul!"

He did not pick himself up by his bootstraps. He did not forge on through sheer will and determination. He leaned on the "blest assurance" that despite struggles as a result of the fallen state of humanity, Christ has regarded our helpless estate and has shed his blood for our souls. Whether dead or alive, those who hold to that hope will truly live. This truth carried Spafford and gave the world the comfort of the hymn. He didn't quit life just because it got hard, and in his case, *hard* would be a grave understatement.

ONE MORE TRY

I would like you to visualize yourself at your current age. What do you see? Now picture yourself five years from now. Do you look like the same person? Have you overcome your struggles? Have you grown as a person? Better question: Do you have a better understanding of who you really are?

If you're doing the same things then that you're doing now, you shouldn't expect any changes in five years. For change to take place tomorrow, we need to do the hard work today. Change is considered a bad thing by a lot of people, but change is a component of growth. Really, it's the catalyst for growth. Therefore, we need to recognize that a modification to our persona in the future requires an active change in the present. That means *now*. What we do today will determine who we will be tomorrow.

Consider some of the things you do now. These things are the breadcrumbs to who you will be. Identify character issues, realize where change needs to happen, and then do it.

What will this look like in your life? Another good question. What if I told you that the answer to this foundational question is right above your head and all you need to do is to reach as high as you possibly can to grasp it?

Go ahead and try it right now. I'm serious, no one's looking. Stand up and reach as high as you can and hold the position for three seconds. Okay, now reach a little higher.

Question: Did you reach a little higher? Whenever I present "The Five and a Half Questions Everyone Must Answer" workshop, roughly 85-90 percent of people are more elevated on the second try. Why? They failed to follow the instructions, which was to reach as HIGH as they could. Remember this; The difference between good and great is often giving it your all, the FIRST time! So many fall short here, not giving their best the first time around. This leads to wasted time and missed opportunities.

Now if you fell short the first time around the best thing to do is learn from your mistake and get it right the next time. Understand this, the difference between success and failure—and yes, excellent and outstanding—is so small. It's the thickness of a centimeter, the "one more" try.

Don't be like the miner who stops hacking rock one inch from striking gold. The difference between success and failure, good and great, is often the "one more" phone call, the "one more" rep, the "one more" interview, the "one more" try, or the "one more" strike.

Despite incredible tragedy, Horatio Spafford always took the next step, fixated on the hope that brought him assurance. Faith keeps the vision and tells you where you're going. But there was also something else Spafford had that enabled him to go on: an unwavering, positive no-quit attitude.

THE INCREDIBLE POWER OF ATTITUDE

Of all the words in the English language, I believe there are (at least) two that are divinely inspired. One is *joy*. Why is it divine? Because it provides God's formula for a successful life (and afterlife). What's the formula? It's simple: **J**esus. **O**thers. **Y**ou. Isn't that awesome? One small word can point to a successful life. Joy differs from happiness in that happiness is circumstantial, while joy is present regardless of what's happening. It's something you always have.

The second word is *attitude*. As human beings, we can control very little. Have you ever thought about that? Attitude is the one thing—actually the *only* thing—you can always control.

While that is powerful enough to make *attitude* divine, there's more. If you write the word on a piece of paper and put the numeric value (for example, A=1, T=20) of each letter under the letter, you'll see something remarkable. Go ahead and try it. Now total it. What did you come up with? If you did it right, it should be 100.

Now do you understand why I believe this to be a divine word? Not yet? Okay, what if I told you that you can never give more than 100 percent to anything you do? Now people will throw around the idea of providing 110 percent effort, but that's impossible. However, it is possible to give 90, 75, or even 50 percent effort to something. So, the fact that *attitude* mathematically equates to 100 is impressive. The perfect number we all can reach, as it relates to attitude.

Noted writer and pastor Charles Swindoll said this about attitude:

> The longer I live, the more I realize the impact of attitude on life. Attitude, to me, is more important than facts. It is more important than failures than successes than what other people think or say or do. It is more important than appearance, gifted-ness, or skill. It will make or break a company, a church, or a home. The remarkable thing is that we have a choice every day

regarding the attitude we will embrace for that day. We cannot change our past. Nor can we change the fact that people will act in a certain way. We also cannot change the inevitable. The only thing that we can do is play on the one string we have, and that is our attitude. I am convinced that life is 10 percent what happens to me and 90 percent how I react to it. And so it is with you—we are in charge of our attitudes.[1]

Our attitude will indeed determine our altitude in all situations. The attitude we approach situations or relationships with is a game-changer, regardless of the circumstances.

WRONG WAY RIEGELS

Roy Riegels was the center for the Cal football team when they played Georgia Tech in the 1929 Rose Bowl. Halfway through the second quarter, Riegels picked up Tech's fumble just thirty yards from the Tech end zone. He then knocked into a tackler, got disoriented, and ended up running sixty-nine yards in the wrong direction!

His own man tackled him at the one-yard line, but the play led to a safety that ended up being the difference between winning and losing. His mistake cost the Bears the game, which finished 8–7. He would forever be known as "Wrong Way Riegels."

What can we learn from this story?

First, we need people around us who will care enough about us to chase us down and stop us from going the wrong way. Sometimes we think we're going in the right direction but need someone to point us to where we need to be going. Riegels's teammate tackled him before he could score for the other team. Do you have people in your life who are willing to stop you in your tracks when they see you going the wrong way? Or are you surrounded with "yes men" or "yes women," friends who only want to see you happy and will tolerate your floundering, your partying, your drinking, your justifications, and your slip-ups—in short, your sin— to an unhealthy extreme?

Second, Roy could've let his mistake negatively define him.

Instead, he refused to allow the name "Wrong Way" to injure him or characterize him. He went on to live a successful life doing vaudeville acts, often making light of his blunder, and turned his mishap into an opportunity to help others tune out the voices that wanted to define them by the name of their mistake. Roy ran in the "wrong" direction. It was a mistake, but consider that his mistake may have pointed him in the right direction after all, awakening him to the possibility of things previously unconsidered.

Then again, sometimes we think we're going in the right direction and need someone to point us to where we need to be going. Wherever you are, I hope this book will help point you in the right direction and encourage you in that old proverb: make lemonade out of lemons. It all depends on how you look at the situation.

It begs the question, how is your attitude?

SIX TYPES OF PEOPLE

Let's start with a 35,000-foot view of who you are right now. I believe there are six types of people in the world, falling into two major categories: The Rearview Mirror and The Front Windshield.

The Rearview Mirror Folks:

1. Type One: You still bathe in old success, living in the bygone "glory days." You are stuck in the past.
2. Type Two: You are haunted by memories of past failures, unable to forgive either yourself or someone else. You are paralyzed.
3. Type Three: You just love to look at yourself. You're consumed with *you* to an unhealthy, unproductive, and damaging degree, both with yourself and in your relationships with others. The world revolves around you.

The Front Windshield Folks:

1. Type Four: You are looking out the front window in a parked car, dazed and confused, unsure of which road to take. You are frozen, indecisive.
2. Type Five: You are looking straight ahead, like a horse with blinders, going one hundred miles per hour, missing things —good things—and essential stop points along the way. You are going to run out of gas, but you don't realize it. You are out of control and unaware of your surroundings.
3. Type Six: Your eyes are wide open to the beauty of God's majesty, taking everything in. Your path is open as far as it needs to be, and even though the distant miles are yet unseen and ambiguous, you're moving forward no matter what. You will take the road as it comes. You are on solid ground.

First, picture the difference in size between the windshield and the rearview mirror affixed to it. One is small and is designed to warn you about what is behind you: those things from the past that we need not fear, but rather learn from. The other is large and is looking toward the open road, the future: what should be your primary focus.

So which type(s) are you? Remember, your "perspective" can be changed!

This illustration brings two powerful verses to mind:

> Let your eyes look straight ahead; fix your gaze directly before you. Give careful thought to the paths for your feet and be steadfast in all your ways. Do not turn to the right or the left; keep your foot from evil.
> — Proverbs 4:25–27

Brothers, I do not consider that I have made it my own. But one thing I do: forgetting what lies behind and straining forward to what lies ahead, I press on toward the goal for the prize of the upward call of God in Christ Jesus.
 — Philippians 3:13–14 ESV

Ultimately, we must put our past behind us to move toward the future. The past is there for us to glean from and reflect on, not stay there or fear it.

WHY SHOULD YOU READ THIS BOOK?

So who are you ... really?

The reality is that you're the only one on earth who knows the answer to that question. Let's be clear. Your current identity has been built based on the sum of your choices to date. Nothing you can do will alter your past, but everything you do going forward will determine your future. Many people deny themselves a purposeful future because they can't let go of the past. You see, understanding your true identity is essential to unlocking the purpose for which you were created—a purposeful identity.

The 5.5 questions that you will tackle in the pages ahead have made all the difference to me, and they can work for you too. Your purposeful identity awaits you! Here we go.

ONE

Question #1 - What Are Your Strengths?

"Do not pray for an easy life. Pray for the strength to endure a difficult one."
— BRUCE LEE

"I can do all this through him who gives me strength."
— PHILIPPIANS 4:13

PLUG IT IN

Imagine coming home after a long day at work and finding a brand-new television sitting in your living room. You didn't buy it and have no clue how it got there. You're amazed, and see a note that reads *A gift for you*. As your heart throbs in wonder, you find your finger already on the power button. Without hesitation, *click*.

Your excitement fades. The TV doesn't work. What would be the first question you would ask? Mine would be, "Why? Why didn't it work?" The answer is simple: you never plugged it in.

Although this television is big, captivating, and extremely valuable, it's worthless if it's not plugged into a power source. Our strengths are the same way. Your *strengths* are the dominant thinking, feeling, and doing patterns that come naturally for you. These include talents, knowledge, and skills. People use these traits and abilities in their daily lives to complete work, relate to others, and achieve goals. They should be the most exercised pieces of our character from day to day.

Unfortunately, too many people have their plug lying on the floor collecting dust. Is yours collecting dust? Are you plugged in? Do you know the power that strengths can have in your life? It's essential that we know our strengths and how to use them, because when we find ourselves in the valleys of life, these strengths are going to be the much-needed tools to help us survive.

Terry Fox was the most-watched athlete on television in Canada two years in a row. He used his strengths to inspire his country and bring hope in the sight of adversity. But who was Terry Fox?

MARATHON OF HOPE

Terry Fox was a Canadian runner with the heart of a lion. He was born to run. He often woke up at four in the morning just to get a couple of miles in before the day started. At the age of eighteen, Terry was accepted into Simon Fraser University. That same year, he found out that his life was about to change. He had cancer. Terry had envisioned himself playing basketball, running, living the entire college experience, but now his mindset was survival.

He had osteosarcoma in his right leg, and it had to be amputated. His family was confused. Why would a young man with so much potential have to face a trial such as this? "Why you? Why you, Terry?" were the only words his brother Fred Fox could fumble out on the day of the operation. Terry's response was, "Why not me?"[1] Strength revealed determination. He was determined to overcome his circumstances, determined to achieve all his goals, determined to defeat self-pity and the bait from the Identity Thief. It's easy to build a home in the valley, but it takes strength to live the life God has chosen for you.

Terry did precisely that. He plugged in. He overcame one of the lowest points in his life and experienced the breakthrough. He won three wheelchair basketball national championships in Vancouver. He was named Companion of the Order of Canada (the youngest person to achieve such an honor at that time). He won the Lou Marsh Award as the nation's top sportsman, and was named Canadian Newsmaker of the Year in 1980 and 1981, but his greatest accomplishment was Marathon of Hope.

The marathon was no easy feat. Marathon of Hope was a five-thousand-mile endeavor across Canada on an artificial leg. It began with Terry dipping his prosthetic leg in the ocean on the easternmost part of Canada; for him, it was Mile Zero. The beginning of the race was the ripple that would become a wave of inspiration over the country.

The first week brought freezing rain, snow, and windstorms, but he set a goal to accomplish a full marathon every single day. Reread that: a full marathon on one leg every single day! At first, no one seemed to notice, but Canada soon saw what was unfolding, and donations began to flood in. Terry ran the marathon for months, pushing his body to its limits.

After 143 days of running, accomplishing 3,339 miles, Terry was forced to halt his run. He noticed his breathing was off, so he stopped and went to a hospital, only to discover his cancer had returned, this time in his lungs. On June 28, 1981, Terry died one month before turning twenty-three.[2]

He never finished the physical run, but he was able to conquer the spiritual run long before the marathon started. The 24 million people who watched, awe-inspired, didn't wish for one leg, but for his grit, bravery, and boldness. Every mile he completed was a mile that built up his character. His determination persisted, overcoming the whispers of doubt that said, "You can't do this," and "People don't care about your cause!" He was selfless, tenacious, and focused, and he had a purpose. It was never just about cancer, but had to do with his being a light to possibility.

He was resilient against all the odds, never complaining or wishing his life different. He plugged in his gift of determination, much like the flat-screen TV, to instill change and hope in his home, Canada. Terry once said, "I'm going to do my very best to make it and not give up. But I might not make it, and if I don't make it, the Marathon of Hope better continue." [3]

We are all running a marathon of hope.

50/50

Terry's story hits home for me. When I see somebody, I see potential. I see pieces of greatness that need assembling for a firm foundation. Sometimes those pieces are not entirely clear, and that can confuse identity and purpose. Now is the time to dig deep and ask yourself, am I using my strengths? Terry had the chance to say no, to throw in the towel and accept defeat. But he said yes. He plugged in determination, courage, and persistence. These traits made all the difference. Before his surgery, he had a 50/50 chance of survival. What if I said you have the same odds to be your best authentic self? A fulfilled self! You have a yes or no chance to do it, and it begins by recognizing your God-given strengths and putting them into action.

Knowledge and wisdom without application are worthless. Knowledge and wisdom with application are *power*. It's time to not only discover your strengths but also learn their purpose in your identity and how they benefit your entire reality. You need to say yes. Yes to a new you, a powerful you, a *purposeful* you. A you who is fully aware of your strengths, firm and not shaken. But it's your choice to make. Living mediocre is hard; standing still is hard. Waking up having mundane days, mundane months, ordinary years is *hard*. One of our greatest assets is our strengths. They open doors, make life exciting, enhance relationships, and carry us out of the valley—but only when exercised.

When we hear 50/50, we typically think of the flip of a coin, heads or tails. Which do you choose? The old saying goes, "Tails never fails." If tails is an ordinary life, never having chased a dream or embraced your strengths, then yes, it never fails. The tails people hit their mark and walk away. Five years from now, they're still in the same place; nothing has changed. *Tails never fail.* I have seen many people walk away from opportunities that could have changed their life, but the tails life is predictable and comfortable. When you choose tails, you miss the chance to plug in your strengths, pursue dreams, and take risks. If you are seeking *average*, then yes, tails never fail. But remember this: nothing great is ever accomplished by being mediocre.

When you choose heads, nothing is guaranteed either, but there's still more than just a chance. Heads choosers don't quit or leave after hitting all tails because there's something rewarding about fighting for a win and seeing its harvest. Strengths allow you to be more productive in your personal and work life; they'll enable you to transform ideas into action and appreciate your real identity. The heads life requires faith because when you hit a dozen tails in a row, it takes determination and persistence to see a victory, that one more try.

What progress have you made? What are some strengths that are unique to you? Here are a couple of tools to help you find out.

TOOL #1: YOUR PERCEIVED STRENGTHS

You probably think there's some big secret to discovering your strengths. No secret. All you need is self-awareness and effort. They are in you right now. Recognizing them is critical. Strengths are your dominant thinking, feeling, and doing patterns. With proper recognition, you can enhance any strength within you. How can you recognize them? Try this:

First, write down what you believe are your strengths.

_____

_____

_____

_____

_____

Next, ask someone who will give you honest feedback what they think of your list. They may tell you that they don't recognize these strengths in you. Ask them why. Then ask them if they see any strengths in you that you're not aware of. Do this with a few people. Be sure the people you ask are ones who love you and have your best interests at heart. Then compare. Once you've discovered some mutual recognition, begin to build on your findings.

There are several other tools that will help you identify your strengths through personality testing. They include Strengths Finder 2.0, DiSC, and Myers-Briggs Type Indicator to name a few. These can help you find your core preferences and patterns for thinking, feeling, and doing. You grow stronger when you spend time in your strengths. By directing all your energy to your strengths, you'll surely get the results you aim for more quickly. (Just keep in mind that there's a difference between skills and strengths. Skills are things that you learn over time, while strengths come naturally.) By focusing on your strengths, you become more efficient, creative, and productive. The byproduct of this is you will be happier and more fulfilled.

So how do you build your strengths? Start by asking yourself what you're doing to grow your strengths on a daily basis. For example:

- What are you reading?
- What are you listening to?
- What are you watching?
- Who are you talking to?
- What are you writing?

IMPORTANT: The content and context are what enables you to grow in your strengths.

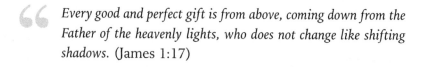

Every good and perfect gift is from above, coming down from the Father of the heavenly lights, who does not change like shifting shadows. (James 1:17)

"Your potential is not based on who you are now or what you did yesterday, but what you're doing now to make you better for tomorrow." (John C. Maxwell)

TOOL #2: THE FIVE FINGERS OF STRENGTH

A great tool to unlock strengths is The Five Fingers of Strengths. This tool uses your own hand as a guide.

1. The Thumb: This is the hands' strongest appendage. The thumb has power.

- Identify the top strengths within you. Use Tool #1.

2. The Pointer: This finger points the way.

- How can you see the greatest strength you possess put into action in the future?

3. The Middle: The middle finger stretches out past all the others, taking risks.

- What risks do you have to take to make your strength a focal point of your life?

4. The Ring: It is quiet but paramount. The ring represents a commitment.

- What do you have to commit to so your strength can grow?

5. The Pinkie: The pinkie is the great equalizer. It completes the hand and helps hold everything together. This finger represents the little things.

- What are the little things you can change today to feed your strengths?

This tool will help you discover hidden strengths that need uncovering. The following tool will expose the habits and routines that are holding you back from progression.

TOOL #3: THE RIGHT SOIL

Where are the places you go to promote your strengths to shine? Michael Jordan's place was the court. Terry Fox's was the road. Who are the people who both encourage you and push you to be the best you? For me, it's my family and an inner circle of men who I know have my back. What I am asking is, what is the right soil that promotes your strengths so they shine?

For some people, it's the library. For others, it's the gym. For others, it's a person, like a coach or friend. Again, you must recognize these places and people in your life so you can thrive. If you ignore or are unaware of your surroundings and influences, it's easy to plant seeds of greatness in the wrong soil and therefore never experience the growth that would have occurred had they been planted in good soil.

Try this simple tool, called The Right Soil:

1. List ten people that influence your time. Then answer these questions:

- Does this person build me up?
- Does this person care about my success?
- What does this person mean to me?

2. List five places you go that *consume* your time. Then answer these questions:

- Does this place inspire me?
- Is this place contributing to my strengths?
- Who else does this place attract?

3. Now, once you've taken an in-depth look at those questions,

ask yourself this: *For my strengths to shine, what is the right soil that promotes just that?*

This tool is universal. You can do it with your spouse, kids, friends, and colleagues—anyone who can help provide the answers you're looking for. The deeper you go, the more your eyes will be opened to who and what places are aiding or hindering your strengths. After completing these tool activities, plug in what you know and watch your strengths grow in power.

THE RIGHT SOIL IN ACTION

A friend of mine shared that he was listening to a podcast about a man who became an overnight success. The jockey brought up his apparent success story, and the man laughed because it reminded him of a time when one of his friends had said the same thing. His success began in college with a decision to separate himself from friends who just wanted to go out and drink. Instead of going out, he dedicated his time to his studies and career goals. In the beginning, his friends begged him to go out and enjoy life; eventually, they faded away and found other buddies to spend their time with. He used his time efficiently and placed his focus on the pathway to success. If he had chosen to go out and drink, he would have given up a massive part of his identity.

Ten years had passed, and he ran into one of those old college drinking buddies. His name by this time was very well known. His friend couldn't help but utter, "Wow, you pretty much became an overnight success, huh?" The guy laughed because nothing was further from the truth. It had taken him ten years of persistence and progress to build his business up. His friend was proud of him and asked him if he wanted to grab a drink at the bar. Ten years later, this friend was still in the same place.

The man took his seeds and planted them in the right soil. His vision, time, and hard work were all enhanced because he surrounded himself with the right people and places. He grew in knowledge, spending weekends at the library, and built relationships with like-minded people who edified him. If he would have spent that time at the bars, the visions and strengths may have sprouted but never blossomed. Maybe he would have become the "regular guy" everyone saw as a dreamer or philosopher. The wrong soil lacks the right nutrition and environment. The friend was a "tails" person. Nothing had changed for him, but for the man who chose to persist, he became an "overnight success." How? Simple: he planted himself in the right soil.

A THOUGHT ON STRENGTH: MY PERSONAL STORY

Persistence. Determination. These became apparent strengths of mine through one of the more spiritually testing times of my life. I was a new Christian, had a passion for baseball, and was ready to combine the two—and I'd a met a man who I thought would be able to help me with this vision.

Dave Branon was the editor of a Christian sports magazine called *Sports Spectrum*. I pitched Dave the idea of having me do some interviews of New York Yankee players for the magazine. Long story short, he helped me get press credentials, and I was able to write some short articles based on several interviews I did. Again I pitched Dave on a new idea: our writing a book together about Christian major leaguers and their faith. He loved the idea and quickly struck a deal with Moody Press to publish the book.

I was no writer, so my role was to go to the stadium and do the interviews on cassette tape. I would then send the tapes to Dave, who would transcribe them and write the actual book. However, there was a challenge: how would I identify the players who were Christians to include in the book? To my good fortune, I had a business friend who was a former New York Yankee, and he handed me what many would call the holy grail of Major League Baseball: *The Major League Baseball Media Guide*. This guide contained highly confidential information about teams and players. I came across something called Baseball Chapel.

Baseball Chapel was the key to my book, or at least where it could begin. It was an organization that commissioned chaplains to conduct small chapels for major- and minor-league baseball teams and to disciple players who sought discipleship. The crazy part was that its headquarters were only fifteen minutes from my house. The executive director, Dave Swanson, had his phone number in the book, so I called him. "Mr. Swanson, I love the Lord and I love baseball," I said. "I'm looking to write a book on Christian players, and I was hoping you could put me in touch with some of them." There was a long silence, and then he said, "Why don't you go ahead and give me a call in three months to discuss this further."

As hard as it was, I agreed to his request. Three months later, I went to my calendar to the day with the red words *Call Dave Swanson*, and did just that. He told me, "Call me in another three months." So I flipped three months ahead in my calendar, marked the date, and hung up the phone. Another three months passed, and it was time to call. He told me the same thing. Call in three months. I was confused and annoyed but still on fire for this book. Now I'm an impatient man, but if Mr. Swanson had the information I needed, nothing was going to stop me from getting it.

Three months later, after a full year had passed, I called Mr. Swanson. He answered and finally agreed to meet at a local diner. I don't remember if I hung up the phone, but I darted up the stairs into the bedroom and changed into a shirt and tie. Within minutes I was standing in front of a tall, imposing bald man with a scowl on his face at the entrance of the diner. "Mr. Swanson?" I asked. He nodded. I went to shake his hand, and he gave me a piece of paper. On it were the names of Major League Baseball players he considered strong Christian men. I could barely believe it. Before we sat down, I asked, "Forgive me, but why now? Why after a year?"

"Take a seat, Joe," Swanson said and smiled. "My family used to own the Thomas' English Muffin company. At one time, I was in charge of purchasing, and whenever a salesman called, I never bought from him the first time. If he came back a second time, I still didn't buy from him, nor did I do so if he came back a third time. But if the salesman *persisted* enough to come a fourth time, then he had a customer for life. You did just that."

This lesson changed my life. I saw the power of persistence. I've seen many people become discouraged when what they're working for doesn't produce fruit immediately. Could you imagine running a marathon on one leg, to wake up and do the same thing the next day? Terry did this for 143 days with cancer in his lungs. He brought in three-quarters of a billion dollars to cancer research. Why did the right soil lead a man to massive success? Why did my calling back for an entire year lead to my first book? The consistent answer across the board is that we all chose to plug in our strengths.

Are you plugged in yet? Are you engaged and committed to discovering and growing your strengths? Make sure you plug them in and use them. We are elevated to the next level when we do this—a level we often can't imagine. However, there's a difference between using and abusing your strengths. Any strength carried to an extreme becomes a weakness.

AN ILLUSTRATION TO REMEMBER: WHEN STRENGTH BECOMES A WEAKNESS

I have a close friend, Eli (names in this story are changed to protect privacy), who was sharing an experience that allowed him to discover one of his strengths. When he was just entering high school and had not a hair on his chin, Eli began seeing his neighbor Shane suffer bullying by a classmate, Bryan. Shane was a bookworm, introverted, and preferred talking to teachers instead of peers. Naturally, it wasn't long before Shane became Bryan's victim. Eli watched this happen for a couple of weeks and realized no one seemed to care that Shane was hurting. Eli did, and it touched his heart; his strength was compassion.

One day, Eli had enough and put Bryan in his place. Eli struck him, bruising his face from his eyebrow to his chin. After seeing the damage, Eli felt great remorse, even compassion for Bryan. But all the other kids who knew Bryan was bullying Shane confirmed that Eli had done the right thing. They were missing compassion, but he reluctantly accepted their affirmations.

From that point on, Eli defended the "little guys," so to speak. For never being a big kid, he was strong and aggressive. Whether it was boxing a 6'7" football player to protect his cousin or pinning one of the school's best wrestlers against the locker for a similar reason, Eli always stepped out to help those who may not have been able to help themselves. What he didn't realize was that self-reason and violence were replacing compassion.

Fast forward three years, and Eli and his crew were on the baseball field behind his house. With a plastic bat, a tennis ball, and a few hats for bases, it was game time. "Peg the Pig" (chucking the ball at the runner as hard as you can to get an out) was allowed for the big kids but not for Logan, a brother of one of the players who was half their age. Logan was good, so they let him play. Eli was up to bat, and Kyle was the pitcher. Kyle had always lived in their trailer park but never seemed to fit in. For some reason, there was always tension between Eli and Kyle.

Kyle unwittingly pegged Logan with the tennis ball, striking the center of his eye socket. Eli was all too ready to "defend the little guy"—or instead, use "defending the little guy" as an excuse to play into his now violent nature. He had completely lost his compassion. With Logan screaming in pain in the background, Eli charged the mound and began to beat Kyle to a pulp. Anyone watching could see the embarrassment on Kyle's face as he pedaled off.

As for Eli, he said, "Joe, I remember chasing him down the road as he flipped me off. I also remember saying, 'Next time! Next time!' I didn't know that I became the bully picking on the kid that didn't fit in."

Well, the next time Eli heard about Kyle, he found out he had committed suicide. After feeling shame for several years, Eli thanks God for bringing light to his eyes and forgiving him for every time he raised a fist. He said, "Caring for the little guy is my strength, but when I thought to care for one and to put my fist to another was right, I became weak."

"Any strength carried to an extreme becomes a weakness."
— Joe Pellegrino

I cannot emphasize enough the blessing of knowing *and* putting your strengths into action. It is a key factor in unlocking God's purpose for your life. Inaction will render you dissatisfied with your life and will negatively affect those people your gifts were meant to help.

One final thought: When someone tells you how great you are, remember that it's your gift from God that's amazing, *not* you.

On to question #2.

TWO

Question #2 - What Are Your Weaknesses?

There's a movie my kids used to watch, Pixar's *A Bug's Life*. In this animated film, a conflict arises between a colony of ants and a gang of grasshoppers led by the uncompromising Hopper. Each summer, because of their fear of the grasshoppers, the ant colony harvests a supply of grain for the grasshoppers, a supply that was meant for the ants themselves.

When a foolish but well-meaning ant, Flick, accidentally knocks over and loses the collected grain into the sea below just moments before the grasshoppers arrive to collect it, there's trouble. The grasshoppers do something they've never done: they confront the ants face-to-face and demand double the grain originally requested to be gathered, in a short period of time. The ants are noticeably intimidated; after all, the grasshoppers are six times their size. They feel helpless to fight against them.

Toward the middle of the movie, our friend Flick stands up to Hopper and takes a beating for it. Afterward there's a scene of all the grasshoppers gathered together joking about the inefficacy of the ants. One grasshopper speaks up and suggests that they just give the ants a break. They have plenty of grain to last them, he notes. Hopper seems to consider this option but brings up the one ant who stood up to him. The other grasshoppers say it was just one puny ant. After a pause, however, Hopper takes a piece of grain and throws it at the suggestive grasshopper. "Did that hurt?" he asks.

The grasshopper laughs and says (and I'm paraphrasing here), "No, of course not."

Hopper throws another grain at him. "What about that?"

Now all the grasshoppers join in laughing. "Nope!"

But when Hopper unleashes the entirety of the grain stored up, it buries not only the suggestive grasshopper, but some of his buddies as well. He says to his fellow grasshoppers, "Those puny little ants outnumber us one hundred to one. And if they ever figure that out, there goes our way of life!"[1]

This story illustrates what I believe to be three distinctive types of weakness: DNA, life-altering experience and character. Let's explore these three types in detail.

DNA

The first type of weakness is DNA weakness. DNA stands for deoxyribonucleic acid; it is the main component of our chromosomes, and therefore is the carrier of genetic information and is present in nearly all living organisms. DNA makes us all different, all unique. No two people are the same. A DNA weakness is something that you are born with, for example, blindness or a missing limb. It is something inherent to you, and it's something that, at best, is extremely difficult to overcome. A DNA weakness is complex and cannot be put into a neat little box. Rather, each DNA weakness needs to be addressed on a per-case basis.

Sometimes an extraordinary person can overcome their DNA weakness out of shear necessity. It takes unbelievable desire, dedication, and discipline to do that. What I'm suggesting is that we understand that DNA is our internal wiring system. It's ok to have a DNA weakness, we all have them and God will use them, if we let Him.

Consider Nick Vujicic. He was born without arms or legs, yet this man has lived a life of inspiration and continues to do so. And when you're born without arms or legs and build one of the most vital ministries in the world, does the length of the straw you were dealt at birth matter as much as what you do with it?

After years of being bullied and attempting to drown himself at a young age, a flash of love changed everything for Nick. He remembered how much his parents loved him. As a result, later in life, he found one of his strengths: speaking this love into the world. Using his significant gift from God, Nick is still encouraging people today. But what could a man without limbs possibly do to inspire the world?

I don't think it matters what any of us believe Nick can do; he's a wonder. The man plays basketball, surfs, skydives, scuba dives, golfs, swims, drives boats, snowboards, and more. Before his thirty-second birthday, he had already acquired a double major, started an international nonprofit and ministry, evangelized to over 400 million people, met seven presidents, spoke at five congressional meetings, written eight books, and the list goes on.

His "overcoming" this DNA weakness didn't mean he miraculously grew arms and legs. It means he had to overcome the mindset of not having them. This was necessary to identify his strengths and put them into action.

He was once bewildered when seeing others jealous of him, a man without limbs. It was as if they now saw the value within the straw regardless of its length. Currently, Nick is still fighting the good fight. He is married and has four children. He is a blessing to the world! How could a man without legs and arms, dealt a catalogue of DNA weaknesses, achieve so much? He credits everything to Jesus. We all have a DNA weakness. Nick's life exemplifies that the unfavorable parts of oneself don't have to define a person. He overcame his DNA weakness, and now that weakness propelled him to fully utilize the strengths God gave him.

 "If God can use a man without arms or legs to be His hands and feet, then God can use you too."
— Nick Vujicic

Yet, DNA weaknesses don't always need to be conquered. Sometimes by focusing on overcoming them, we waste precious time that could have been spent on our strengths and gifts.

When I was in college, I wanted to be a rock star. I couldn't play an instrument, so the only thing I could do was be a lead singer. The challenge was that I don't have a good singing voice, even for rock. Oh, I tried my best, but every time I sang, the dogs would start to howl. (Okay, maybe it wasn't that bad, but you get the point.) In fact, I needed to shake off that dream and focus on the areas that I could expect to find success in, developing my strengths and putting them into action.

Regardless, it is still important to recognize this type of weakness. Why? Because our DNA weaknesses can either limit or propel us.

LIFE-ALTERING EXPERIENCE

There's an initial feeling that hits us like an ice-cold plunge into deep waters upon receiving tragic news. A plunge that can easily leave the receiver of such news feeling befuddled, lost, or perhaps reflexively swimming around in circles – in motion, but actually going nowhere! Often following the arrival of unexpected and unwelcome news, the hearers commonly experience a state of prolonged mental shock (PTSD is a well-known example of this). These moments of anguish are often hard to overcome; it can be even more challenging to recognize the long-lasting effects that they can have on a person's life. What I am referring to is the second type of weakness a person can face in their lifetime- the profound impacts of a life-altering experience.

What is a life-altering experience? In the context of this book I am defining a life-altering experience as the following – an unforeseen moment that changed your entire outlook on life, and which in turn, had negative implications for your future. Some typical examples include, going to war and seeing death for the first time, contracting a serious disease, losing a limb in the middle period of your life, or even losing a loved one without warning. I believe that these traumatic and painful events can lead us to one of the most important weaknesses for anyone to identify, and we will endeavor to do so here.

There are a few stories I think of that come to mind when I think about these life-altering experiences. The first one concerns a man who lost his wife years ago. My friend Craig was sharing the story with me the other day and it is heartbreaking. Not only is it hard to hear about anyone who loses a loved one but the tragic effect it had on this man's life makes it that much harder.

The man shared with Craig how that after losing his wife, things were just never the same. Even though he remarried, had a child, and tried to get past what had happened, he could never seem to find peace after that fateful event. His second marriage eventually ended in divorce, his son (with whom he has a good relationship) lives several hours away, and the man lives alone. The memories of his military days and the loss of his wife many years ago have had lasting, negative effects on his life. Since losing his own father just a couple years ago, he has only grown colder inside. It seems as though an air of melancholy follows him wherever he goes. The man said something to Craig that reveals his deep sense of grief, "After 26 years, and visiting her grave twice a week, I just don't see how anyone can get over losing the love of their life." This was truly a life-altering experience for this man. Many try to cope with these losses in a negative way - some "drown their sorrows" in alcohol, others may seek escape in drugs, pornography, workaholism, and so on. The recent rise of the opioid epidemic is but one symptom of this deep inner void felt by thousands, the sad aftermath of deep traumas, that have not been properly dealt with, and resolved.

A second story also hits home. This one is about a British soldier named William, who fought in what is referred to as The Troubles – a three-decade conflict between the nationalist and unionist factions in Ireland. He suffers from PTSD. He says he and his eight troops had to march through the streets of Ireland, always on guard against an impending attack. "Knowing that those eight guys had my back, was amazing. There was no question that any one of us would willingly give our life for the next guy. We were brothers." He goes on to say that this certainty of having another person willing to fight alongside him gave him comfort. Still, as the conflict continued many things were seen, disturbing things, and other haunting scenes that would stay with him for a long time to come. One of the effects that the war had on him is called Post-Traumatic Stress Disorder – this has been his life-altering experience.

He humbly speaks about the challenges this has given him in his life but more than the trouble he speaks to a hope he has. Since the war, and especially recently, he has had a growing desire to reignite his relationship with Jesus. He says there came a point where he had drifted away from faith in his younger years, but now is rediscovering the love of Christ. He is hoping to eventually buy a bus, remodel it, and give homeless veterans a place to sleep and live.

A third story that comes to mind is that of an atheist named John. This man went to school and became a scientist of some sort. He didn't believe in God nor did he care to investigate anything about him. He thought life was simply about living a good life, doing good by other people, and taking care of your family, and as far as he was concerned, God wasn't needed in order for him to do those things. John's wife was very much on the same page. They were the couple that had a plan, and after accomplishing just about all they had sought out to, found themselves at odds. With what? An empty feeling. They thought for a while about what might be able to fill this emptiness, this gap in their life. The answer became obvious: to complete the "live a good life" check list, the next item was to have a child. Well, they began trying. It wasn't long until John and his wife were able to hold their very own baby. He says the moment he wrapped his arms around the child something special happened, something profound spoke to him about the wonderful gift that he held tenderly in his arms.

This child had begun to change their lives. John was falling in love with their family's new arrival, and life was changing. But suddenly, it was changing too fast. One day after work, he found himself confronted by a confusing scene as he pulled in front of the babysitters' residence. He was shocked when he saw an ambulance parked out front, and by the additional sight of the babysitter standing outside of the door, crying profusely. John ran up to see what was going on. The babysitter told him that she put his son down for a nap and that the child mysteriously didn't wake up. His son was only eight months old when he died. The news was too much to bear for John. I can only imagine the artic chill that must have gone through his body. He explains the heartache, the sadness, the brokenness that came with the news. What happened next?

Suddenly, John felt an unexplainable urge to go to church. He needed an answer as to why this would happen and what he was to do. That night at the church the message was about how to deal with loss. John says the message was so specific to what he was going through that it was as if the Pastor was speaking directly to him. Not long after that, John surrendered to God's Call to become a Pastor. Now he speaks about how the love of Jesus has healed his broken heart, provided the deepest answers he needed, and has given him hope to be reunited with his son one day.

Each of these people have found themselves shaken by some of the toughest battles that this life has to offer. These battles always leave scars and often hurt the soldiers who have had to live through them. For some people they become a life crippling experience. Everyone must know that undealt with, these experiences can give rise to an inescapable weakness in your life. To the Veteran who lost his wife and any readers who are wondering how you can overcome a life-altering weakness, I say this, it is possible to find hope. There is a way to overcome these seemingly unanswerable weaknesses. John and Bill found their answer in the love of Jesus. If you are at odds today with an unresolved issue from your past, I urge you to seek answers. For those who seek, it will be found.

. . .

CHARACTER

The third type of weakness is character weakness. These are the weaknesses we must change. If we want to be the person God crafted us to be, we must recognize our flaws and learn to correct them. Our personal qualities don't have to hinder our growth; they are not permanent. A character weakness can start as a negative aspect of your persona. Unidentified, it can grow into a persona in and of itself. That's when a character weakness becomes dangerous to one's purposeful identity. To overcome such weaknesses, they first need to be identified. Look how this truth hit my friend Craig.

He told me, "My son enjoys watching his mother vacuum. He observes in awe as this machine sucks up the Cheerios he had spilled during snack time. As he became more curious, he realized the cord was the source of its power. Sure enough, he took matters into his own hands and tried plugging the cord into the outlet. I saw what was happening and quickly smacked his hand and yelled at him. He was instantly upset, crying and not understanding what was going on. I used aggression and authority to discipline my son. I hurt him, physically and emotionally. And do you know what he did? He turned to me for a hug for comfort. There was no resentment; he just wanted me. I have learned that discipline does not have to come from a place of anger but a place of love. All I wanted was to protect him, but how I went about it did not reflect my care and concern. I needed to learn my son's perspective as a toddler. He was thinking, wondering, and having an understanding of the vacuum. I disrupted a moment of discovery with aggression, and in turn, both my son and I were affected."

This example shows how character weaknesses are damaging and how, to be overcome, they must be identified and unplugged. Could you imagine if Craig never recognized how that was destructive? He thought anger and aggression were vital tools for discipline; it turns out they only go so far. Sooner or later, his son would shut him out and not trust him.

When I was a kid, I got pushed around in school. Not that much, but even one time was enough for me to want to become the big guy rather than the little one. In becoming the big guy, I used a piece of my character that I never needed to use, and as the old traditional saying goes, "if you don't use it, you lose it." Well, I lost it—my integrity. On my way to becoming the "man," I became an incorrigible liar. My integrity went out the window.

As a kid, I'm not sure if I could have identified the hole in my character. This much is true: whether it's a hole in our tire, shoe, or heart, none of us like the feeling of emptiness. God has given us a natural inclination to fill the void in our lives, but without seeing that He is the solution, we all will use whatever is around us to fill the holes. It was a catch-22. The more I lied, the more the gap grew. The deeper the hole, the more filling it needed.

So instead of becoming aware of the compulsive tendencies I was plugging into, I became glib. Going into college, I chose to redefine who I was. The lies continued to fill this hole in my character. I became the outspoken kid who was quick to share what I thought. The only thing bigger than my head was my ego, and the only thing bigger than my ego was my head. This was the new me. The new me was likable. The new me was cool. The new me was good at what he did. The new me was … well, hollow.

When I finished college, I quickly landed a job at a major corporation where I spent the next two years of my life. Then I knew it was time to move on, as I had aspirations of starting my own company. But I also knew I needed more seasoning, which I believed I could garner from working for a smaller company. So I found a headhunter to find me just the right position. The first interview he got me changed everything. I strolled in, a bit nervous but on the outside appearing cool as ice. My nerves relaxed when I saw the interviewer wasn't much older than I was.

Five minutes into the conversation, we connected. So much so that at one point I remember throwing my feet up on his desk and my hands behind my head as I talked about the college party days. It was a good interview, and I left him with a firm handshake and a cunning smile that only two college buddies would understand.

When I returned home, there was a message on my answering

machine from my headhunter. He called to inform me that I didn't get the job. At first, I didn't understand. We had hit it off almost on a "spiritual" level. This guy was going to be my boy. But it all made sense when the headhunter finished and said, "By the way, he asked me to give you a message: grow up!" *Smack!* I was blindsided. He had been testing me.

Someone had brought my weakness to light. My moral deficiency was exposed. Up to this point, it had been masked by a silver lining. However, the silver lining was beginning to fade, and I was facing exposure. All along, I thought my alter ego was building me up, but it was breaking me down. I decided I needed to change, to grow up. I was ready to overcome this hurdle and embrace my *real* character.

The root cause of character weakness can be traced directly to pride, arrogance, or self-interest, just to name a few negative traits. We all need to address these traits. They are non-negotiables, and like DNA weaknesses, they require great discipline to overcome. To overcome a character weakness, you're going to need support. Brothers and sisters, mentors and friends, whoever, to stand alongside you and hold you accountable. People are the key to discovering and changing a character weakness.

TOOL #4: FIND A FRIEND

Character weaknesses and life-changing experiences can pose a severe threat to our true identity if we allow them to take root. One of the best ways I have found to unplug such weaknesses is by having someone that I can share my burdens with, a person who holds me accountable to change—a friend.

I know many of us would rather skip that part. We don't want to waste time on improving a part of ourselves that we can easily keep hidden. Sometimes we are afraid to think about what has happened in the past. The result is internalizing thoughts, feelings, and struggles, and a tendency to travel the road alone when, on either side, there are people who are willing to help. Our journey toward purposeful identity doesn't have to be isolated; we should not detach from each other. So reach out and ask a friend to keep you accountable. Take it from me. It's a daily battle, a continual surrender, when it comes to character weakness or a life-altering experience. Every day we fight to lay down our pride, our lying, our cheating, our wandering eyes, the troublesome grip of the past. I am grateful for my friends who have been there for me, to listen and keep me in the fight.

TOOL #5: HEALTHY WEAKNESS AWARENESS FORMULA

WHAT ARE MY WEAKNESSES, REALLY?

The truth will set you free, so let's get to it. The world is the Identity Thief's playground. Moment after moment, he will lie, try to intimidate you and hide your purpose from you, discourage you, and destroy any attempt you make at progress. One look at the Terry Fox and Nick Vujicic stories, and you know what I'm saying. A place where the Identity Thief can't reside is in a place of honesty. One thing he does want is for us to believe that our weaknesses are irreversible. However, when our strengths are working together in concert, our shortcomings are more easily overcome.

Simply put, for us to recognize our weaknesses, we must first be honest with ourselves. Then we need to engage our strengths so that we can be overcomers. Let's make some progress and figure out a weakness or two.

When asking ourselves about a weakness, we can either be honest or dishonest, constructive or destructive. The formulas below are designed for a person who is taking an active introspective and extrospective look at their self-weaknesses - be they DNA, life-altering, or character. Like the previous tools, where you investigated your strengths, the sole purpose of this tool is to help you identify your weaknesses.

There is a problem, however. People typically don't like recognizing weaknesses. Some will avoid recognition at all cost and obtain a delusional perspective on what their real weaknesses are, never truly being able to pinpoint what weaknesses need attention. Others hyperinflate their weaknesses and in the process become unjustifiably depressed because they allow self-pity into the equation. It is always wise to avoid self-pity.

There are four formulas listed below, but only one works for sure, kind of like the parable Jesus used about the seed sower and the four different types of soil. He laid out each path and the result of each one to avoid, but he also revealed the right path and soil to plant seeds in.

Step 1

The first thing to do is list as many perceived traits, skills, interests, goals, visions, etc. that you want to review about yourself. Then ask if they are a weakness and follow the formula outlines to get a true answer. (Hint: Doing this activity with someone who knows you well may yield better results.) Here are the possible formulas when asking yourself about weaknesses.

Step 2

Ask + Dishonest with Oneself = Delusional Weakness Awareness

It is delusional because, from the beginning, dishonesty with self has polluted the person's ability to see reality purely.

An example of this could be a star running back who wants to play quarterback but constantly ignores his inaccuracy and poor arm strength, all while telling himself he is good and getting better despite no true progress.

Ask + Be Honest with Oneself + Embrace Self-Pity = Depressing Weakness Awareness

Being honest with oneself about weaknesses takes humility and is good, but dwelling on them is unmotivating, deflating, dispiriting, and depressing. Finding and sustaining progress amid a depressed attitude would be a daunting task.

An example of this would be a college student who fails five chemistry exams in a row. If he is honest, he will determine he is not doing well in chemistry. If he allows self-pity in and views chemistry with an attitude like "Dang, I'm going to fail this course, but it doesn't matter because it's just too tough for my limited mind to comprehend," he will miss the opportunity to improve and save his GPA.

Ask + Be Dishonest with Oneself + Embrace Self-Pity = Destructive Weakness Awareness

When it comes to weakness, if you're dishonest with yourself, then a lie can quickly become destructive. For instance, an all-star quarterback could begin to question his ability if he started throwing a few incomplete passes during practice. This is different from the running back because the quarterback's skill has already been realized by the coaches. Now, pressure to perform and worry about failing affects the QB. He starts asking if he's really any good or if he's surrounded by hype-men. Feelings of doubt infiltrate his confidence, stunting his growth. If he decides to dwell on those emotions and picks apart his game, all the work his coaches are doing to build up a big-time player could be lost. If the star athlete remains in this pressure zone, he may very well find he naturally steps away from his calling and loses a huge piece of his identity in the process. The result is a destructive weakness awareness.

Ask + Be Honest with Oneself + Avoid Self-Pity = Healthy Weakness Awareness

This is the only formula that will ultimately benefit your awareness of your weaknesses.

Now let's take a look at the full procedure in action.

HEALTHY WEAKNESS AWARENESS FORMULA

Imagine you just opened your first business. It's been a long time coming, a dream you've had since you were a teenager. You make wooden bats, crafted from the best maple and ash billets; your product is durable and first rate. The orders have been flooding in, but you're struggling to figure out the accounting details. Numbers have never been your strong suit. You don't want to ask for help because you want others to think you know it all, which is *pride*.

Step 1: Be Honest

Bookkeeping and records are your weaknesses. That doesn't mean you're a lousy business owner; it means you need help and guidance when it comes to the financials.

Step 2: Avoid Self-Pity

Ward off the lies you tell yourself—that you won't make it, that you aren't smart enough, and that you can't learn. Enroll in a business course, make your way to the Better Business Bureau, or ask your brother-in-law who has a business degree.

When you have healthy weakness awareness, the possibilities are endless. This example shows that when the two parts of the equation *Be Honest + Avoid Self-Pity,* are applied, our character and situation are enhanced. The other equations always take something away, be it hope, determination, or truth. You pick the one you want but remember this: how you approach your weaknesses can stop you in your tracks or propel you forward. If you can, be honest with yourself or take the honesty of a friend while avoiding self-pity. You then will be able to view your weakness as an opportunity for growth.

A THOUGHT ON WEAKNESS: A PERSONAL STORY OF OVERCOMING

While all of us have DNA weaknesses, sometimes it's good that we do. Staying focused on your strengths rather than trying to change something in your DNA can change your life. Now, if you receive a calling to overcome them, then for the glory of God, do it! Still, it's essential to know that unplugging character weakness (doubt, fear, worry) and plugging in strengths are essential to overcome a DNA weakness.

Not everyone can identify weaknesses, let alone change them. Breaking through a life-altering experience needs much introspection and willful action to overcome. While overcoming DNA weaknesses needs a strong character. Either way, being able to see personal flaws and being aware enough to make changes is grace at work. Through humbling experiences - some life-altering - and revelation from God, I have been able to identify weaknesses in my life. God led me to a vision called Legacy Minded Men and other ideas, including books I wanted to write. However, a piece of me knew that I wasn't a proficient writer—a weakness. Guess what? I only knew that because I accepted honesty. I could have lied, but the result would have led to years of self-justifications as to why I hadn't written the books. Here's what I did: I decided to be open to what I knew, which was:

I have a vision from God to write books. I'm not a natural-born writer.

My situation reminded me a little of Moses and Aaron. Moses was a poor speaker, but God called him to lead the chosen people out of Egypt. How does a man with a speech impediment lead millions of people? First, it's important to mention that God's chosen people were being led from a life of slavery, and Moses wasn't a slave by any means. Instead, he lived a luxurious life, raised as the son of Pharaoh's daughter. This fact is critical to how he would approach the Israelites (the chosen people). They would naturally resent him, and perhaps not even listen at all. How could they? Moses didn't know the struggles of being a slave.

Now Moses had two walls to climb over: he had a significant speech impediment, and a significant gap in life experiences as compared to the people he would lead. Well, God directed Moses to his brother, Aaron, who was a great speaker and could directly relate to the oppression of the Israelites, being a slave himself. Moses was able to be confident in relaying messages from God, through Aaron, to the people.

It was easy for me to make a big decision: the books are getting written! I unplugged my weakness, be it self-doubt, inability, or fear. What I did was find other men whose strengths complemented my weakness, and together we delivered God's message. It's that simple. I was honest with myself, knew something about myself, and moved forward. Weaknesses don't stop us in our tracks. How we approach them is what matters.

"Give God your weakness, and he will give you his strength."
— Anonymous

AN ILLUSTRATION TO REMEMBER: FAULTY VISION

One of the biggest weaknesses of all is a faulty vision. Often, we get so focused on what's at the top of the mountain that we forget to look around during the climb. It can become dangerous when we seek worldly desires and dreams, such as the house with the white picket fence, the brand-new truck, and all the expensive "toys." You can work yourself to death attaining these "dreams," and, as a result, miss out on the little moments that mean the most. Like your child's first home run, which you saw on a video because you were working at the office. Like your dad's sixtieth birthday party you saw through your wife's Facebook photos because you were out of town for a business meeting.

You see, a significant weakness of ours is that we strive to make it to the top, only to discover that we missed what was *really* important: moments we can never get back. I'm not saying you shouldn't work hard. I'm simply saying don't sacrifice the climb, because as you are climbing, you can create genuine moments of happiness and love. When we overcome the weakness of faulty vision, then we get to be present.

When you decide to make this change, you can begin to focus your energy on your physical, mental, and emotional well-being. The Lord says it perfectly: "Be still, and know that I am God" (Psalm 46:10).

You must learn to put on the brakes and seize the moment! When you squash the weakness of living in the faulty vision, something remarkable happens: you receive your purposeful identity.

Proverbs 19:21 says, "Many are the plans in a person's heart, but it is the Lord's purpose that prevails." Focus on the *now*. Focus on *God*. *Be* in the moment. Understanding that the greatest joys in life do not come from planning for the future or worrying about what is going to happen next, but about loving and being grateful for the present moment, is pivotal. Living in the now puts the control in God's hands; it allows us to surrender our weaknesses so that we can have complete vision.

"Where there is no vision, there is no hope."[2]
— George Washington Carver

WEAKNESS BRINGS US TOGETHER

We are relational people. We were created to work and interact with each other. That is the body of Christ, the ideal model for human existence. Not everybody is meant to be at the pulpit. Not everybody is meant to play an instrument. But everybody is meant to play a part. Our job is to find out what that part is and put it into action.

Allow me to use myself as an example. I've co-authored five books. Now here's the interesting thing about these books: I didn't write any of them. My name is on every one of these books, but I didn't write them. I knew that God gave me a word that I needed to capture, but I didn't have the ability to write effectively. So what I did was find somebody whose strength was my weakness. A writer. Now I have four co-authors of my five books. I could have said, "I can't do this because I can't write," but I didn't want to let that stop me, because the purpose that God was revealing to me was too important to let fall by the wayside.

What's stopping you from letting out the greatness that's in you? It's not enough to know your strengths and to know your purpose.

You have to identify your weaknesses and be aware of them so they don't become roadblocks along your path.

We are puny little ants in our weaknesses. We are. And there are those who would like to keep us that way, namely the greatest enemy of God: Satan. Let's jump back to the opening illustration. Hopper didn't want the ants to find out that if they banded together, they could be something, do something, be stronger. I hope that you can see what Hopper spent the entirety of the movie trying to keep the ants from knowing: that there is strength in weakness. Spoiler alert!

The ants *do* finally realize that they're stronger together, and they squash the heck out of Hopper.

A FINAL THOUGHT

Want to succeed? Feed your strengths and understand and manage your weaknesses!

THREE

Question #3 - What Are You Passionate About?

"There is no passion to be found playing small—in settling for a life that is less than the one you are capable of living."
— NELSON MANDELA

"A great leader's courage to fulfill his vision comes from passion, not position."
— JOHN C. MAXWELL

INTRODUCTION TO PASSION

P assion wakes you up, gets you going, and *keeps* you going. It prepares you for the adventure of a lifetime. It never sleeps, never quits, and always pursues. Passion fuels the father to work two jobs to put his children through college. It drives the athlete to train before the sun rises. It compels the pastor to prepare for hours before delivering his Sunday sermon.

In Scripture, Paul urged his readers to live a passionate life through the love of Jesus Christ:

Dear Corinthians, I can't tell you how much I long for you to enter this wide-open, spacious life. We didn't fence you in. The smallness you feel comes from within you. Your lives aren't small, but you're living them in a small way. I'm speaking as plainly as I can with great affection. Open up your lives. Live openly and expansively! (2 Corinthians 6:11–13 MSG)

Do you see how enthused Paul was to help transform the lives of others? That's passion. It makes your heart pound and evokes a love so intense that it forces you to act. When you act on a justified passion, you become productive, and this productiveness yields results, which in turn leads to fulfillment. With that in mind, may I suggest that there are two types of passions: internal and external. Let's explore the two.

INTERNAL PASSION: GETTING THE ENGINE GOING

Billy Graham once said, "Live each day as if it were your last, for someday it will be."[1] What a powerful statement. And what better way is there to live than pursuing our passions. The first step is to ask the question, what gets my engine going? The heart is the engine where you'll find internal passion; knowing what starts it up is the key. It may be sports, theater, selling cars, preaching, cooking, reading, or even mowing lawns. Internal passion is what exhilarates us, tells "tired" to take a back seat, and awakens us with a heart pounding.

Tony, an old friend of mine, told me a story about a friend of his who loved mowing lawns. A humble man with few amenities who had a passion for maintaining properties decided to start a business and become a greenskeeper. He started small, like most business owners. Tony watched his friend work hard for several years. Well, within a few years, this man turned his little mowing business into a multimillion-dollar enterprise. There is no doubt the man's engine ignited from seeing beautifully maintained landscapes. When we pursue the passion God has placed in our heart, success follows. But only when we act on it.

In America, I see a society that revs its engine on materialism, vanity, and self-righteousness. Some only care for themselves: "I want this, this, this, this, and, oh yeah, that too." These desires typically require little effort to fulfill. People like this are what I call the "to and fro'ers." They go to work, then back home. They go to the store, then back home. They go to the bar, then back home. The car (symbolically speaking) they need to get the job done is a Fiat 500. A low 135-horsepower is enough for them, and in fact, they often believe that's all their engine has, but that's just not true. We can do so much more! The reason this has become such a phenomenon is that too often, people don't take the time to look into what gets their motor running, which is sad. Why? Because when our passions and strengths intersect, it usually points to purpose, and that's where we all want to be.

It is essential to ask these questions: "Is this the limit of my potential?" and "If today were my last day on earth, would I be engaged in the pursuit of my passion?" Well, if your passion is just to accumulate more stuff, then I certainly hope not. But if your passion is something that not only puts a smile on your face but also helps others, now *that's* the way to go!

Unfortunately, a good number of people are falling into the trap of the Identity Thief, being content with the monotony of life. Their chosen path requires no growth, no risk, no desire. Naturally, people avoid things that need more energy and effort than they believe they have. But what if I told you there is more—a life as fast and exhilarating as a 430-horsepower Chevy Corvette. Where would you go then?

Internal passion ignites, excites, and makes life worth living. Pursuing what you know you love leads to a life where the days build up to weeks, months, and years of satisfaction. Ultimately, when the tribulations of life find you, and they will, the Fiat 500 is not the vehicle you want to be driving. But the good news is that's *not* your true engine!

Perhaps you believe or have been told that you're somehow like the owner of that Fiat 500. Well, today is trade-in day, because you're leaving the garage in a brand-new candy-apple-red Corvette. The real deal. Any dream, vision, hope, desire, or internal passion is achievable in this ride. It's essential to have internal forces that are powered by a vision and a yearning desire to answer the call, because these are what will reveal our true horsepower. The goal isn't just knowing our internal passion, it's knowing and then acting on it. Few people do. What about you?

EXTERNAL PASSION

I would like my old childhood friend, Popeye the Sailor, to introduce the second type of passion. Do you remember some of the things Popeye used to say? How about "I am what I am"? Or maybe you've heard this one: "I've had all I can stands, and I can't stands no more!" It's as though he's saying, "It breaks my heart, and I'm going to do something about it."

What breaks your heart? Many people know what it is that gets them going and out of bed. They may even know the things that break their heart. The most crucial step is taking action every day to see such heartaches lessen. People like Abe Lincoln, Nelson Mandela, and Martin Luther King Jr. are all men who acted from a broken heart. They saw injustice and people hurting, and leaped into action without thinking about themselves. It gnawed at them, pushed them, awakened them, and broke them, and they knew the only way to fix it was action. External passions don't necessarily have to make us become social revolutionaries, but that's one obvious example.

I've seen dads working two jobs drop everything to make sure they're at their little girl's soccer game, and moms who work from dusk till dawn just to put a hot meal on the table—something they may not have had growing up. Many parents feel this external passion for dedicating all they have so their children can live better lives than they did.

The examples are endless. Whether it's creating a documentary on sex trafficking or giving a sandwich to a homeless person, when you step out and act on your passion, expect the Identity Thief to swoop in. Mark my words: the day you discover what breaks your heart, is going to be the same day you'll feel a significant push to "do it tomorrow." This is no accident, regardless of the time and place you find out.

Some people put off getting into the action because they're being swayed by subtle thoughts that emanate from the Identity Thief. Eventually, they become so influenced by these thoughts that the very thing they're passionate about eventually becomes somewhat of an obstruction to their "comfortable" life. Over time, the external passion that once moved their heart becomes like an unwanted knick-knack lying around the living room. Every time they sit down and toss their feet up on the coffee table, it's there. When they vacuum, it's there. When they have friends over, it's there.

Eventually, the person who has been numbed by the Identity Thief can't take it anymore and puts their passion on the top shelf of the closet. They wait and wait and wait to move on it, holding out for the right day to pull it down and finally do what would make them feel fully alive. But they're treating an external passion as if it were an umbrella. "Umbrellas are only good for specific days, and one day will be the right day to use it" is the typical thought. Procrastination sets in—and for the moment, the Identity Thief has won!

To illustrate, maybe you have put your deep compassion for the elderly on the shelf. Let's say that one day, at a local coffee shop, you overhear a man in line telling his friend how much he misses his wife of forty-six years who died of cancer. Your heart breaks at the sadness in his voice. You want to interject and provide a word of encouragement, but you don't. A few days pass, and you see an older woman struggling to put her groceries in her car, and once again, your heart breaks. You realize how difficult everyday demanding tasks must be for her. But you never actually walk over to help her load her groceries.

You see, when you put the unwanted knick-knack away, conveniently out of sight, you pay a price: you've become disconnected from your external passion. At that point, you half-heartedly hope that someone else will step in and take action. It's as though you find yourself watching from behind the window, passively waiting for the rainy day—that is, the day to finally pull out that umbrella and act. But unless you're intentional, that day will never come.

When you give up on a passion, you walk away from an opportunity to make a difference. What a tragedy to believe that someone else can and will take action to stop something that breaks *your* heart. It can be the thrill of a lifetime to discover your external passion, but it won't come without a cost. Therefore, passion is defined as not just what we love but what we are willing to suffer for.

What breaks your heart? What causes you to jump into other people's conversations? What ignites a fire in your soul? It might be world hunger, orphans, alcohol abuse, depression, sex trafficking, or racism. So many foundations begin with a breaking heart because they just "can't stands it no more," as Popeye used to say.

For me, seeing men who have lost their way and have no apparent direction triggers my external passion and moves me to action. That's why I started Legacy Minded Men, a ministry that helps "Transform lives by engaging, equipping and encouraging men to build a Christ-centered Legacy." I love it! What are *your* external passions? Can you identify them? And if you know what they are, have you been acting on them?

If not, ask yourself why.

PUTTING THEM TOGETHER

God has a way of speaking to us, even in subtle ways. There are times when I pass the cemetery that my stomach turns and my heart gets heavy, and not because it's a place of death. No. What I think about is all the star athletes, the amazing teachers, the quick-witted comedians, and the brilliant inventors who never walked out their callings. I'm thinking of the best-tasting sandwiches, the much-needed serums, and the life-aiding inventions that could have made such an impact for the good of humanity. But because of inaction, it was all buried with them, never seeing the light of day. What a shame. What a crime. My heart aches knowing what could have been.

It doesn't make sense. I sometimes ponder questions: How could such a great mind not create that life-giving serum? How could a talented little girl not hit the Broadway stage? This question goes deep down to the roots of our society. That little girl never thought she could because she grew up poor and had never seen a real-life example of success, only a father who worked hard during challenging times just to barely make it by—or worse, no father at all. How could *she* ever hope to make it?

What about pre-med students who abandoned their field because they received painful criticism and shame for making mistakes. No matter how old you are, it's never too late to be an example. That's true for encouraging someone else to chase their passion, just as it is for you to go out there and act on your own passions. Be relentless in your journey and promote relentlessness to those you see with hope in their eyes. Unfortunately, this world is not going to play nicely, and the Identity Thief has that reality going for him. We might as well have the support of each other going for us.

Whether it's an internal passion (something you love) or an external passion (something that breaks your heart), it was given to you because someone out in the world needs to see it. People need it because the life lived—the hall of fame football player, for instance—gives hope to the life wanting to live, the young kid with a dream.

I have been up and down on the roller coaster of life, and God indeed has spoken subtly to me, but not so subtly that I can't hear Him. I know that's true for you too. The best thing we can do is ask and listen. Ask and listen. Ask and listen. He will reveal. Now is the time to act. Answer the call and do what you love or what breaks your heart. Time has never been on our side. Think it is? Just look at the cemetery. How many of those serums have gone unmade? How many poems never made it onto a page? How many beautiful voices have never been heard?

 "Many people die with their music still in them. Too often, it is because they are always getting ready to live. ... Before they know it ... time runs out."
— Oliver Wendell Holmes

TOOL #6: 5 TIPS FOR PASSION

Here are some tips for discovering your passion:

1. **Always be hungry to learn.** Life can change in a minute, so when it comes to knowledge, take it in. The more you know about you, the more you know what you like or dislike.
2. **Always be humble.** As we pursue our passions, success will follow. You'll get good at the things you love. It's inevitable because we don't give up on what we love. The important thing is to stay humble and remember to never to misuse a gift.
3. **Never settle.** Always give your best effort. Don't settle for less!
4. **Take the chance.** You indeed miss 100 percent of the shots you don't take. Be willing to take a chance on yourself. You have a great Partner on your side who wants to see you successful, but you have to take a chance and want it.
5. **If you fail, learn the lesson.** Failing isn't a bad thing. In my experience, I must say that nothing has taught me, and the professionals around me, more than our failures. Not learning from failure is what's bad. From our very first steps, to our journey through school, and finally to the career world, we have all failed at one time or another. But why did that determined baby get up and try again—and again—even after a fall? Because failure was teaching that little one a lesson: "If you want to get over to Mom or Dad, you're going to have to want it!"

TOOL #7: THE PASSION QUIZ

When it comes to our passions, we need to realize that they take effort, risk, and productivity. In your own life, where do you see yourself sacrificing time, money, energy? Maybe on the weekends, you spend your time watching sports when you could be pursuing your passion for coaching. If you're willing to sacrifice hours watching football highlights, then you can apply that time to, say, coaching. Ask yourself these questions and see if your passions reveal themselves to you:

- What am I hungry for?
- Why is it important to be humble?
- Have I settled?
- What is blocking me from finding my passion?
- What do I love doing (internal passion)? List 3 things.
- What breaks my heart (external passion)? List 3 things.
- What am I willing to sacrifice to make my passion a reality?
- What am I willing to invest in my passion?
- If today were my last day to live, what would I do?

A THOUGHT ON PASSION: LIVING WITH PASSION

I pray these words most days: "Lord, give me wisdom. Give me knowledge. Give me the discernment to know how to implement them."

You see, opportunities abound every day, and each of us have things to be passionate about, decisions to be made, and roads to pursue. I deal with people with problems all the time. I deal with people who have great challenges, on top of dealing with difficulties and obstacles in my own life. Without the discernment to know how to implement God-given wisdom and knowledge, the life roads we travel can easily become winding, narrow, and quite bumpy, and eventually even lead to a dead end.

I have a burning passion for Jesus Christ and sharing his redemptive power with the world, which is my external passion, but without knowing him, I could have never figured out my internal passion for speaking. We need a healthy dynamic between our passions, personal life, and spiritual walk with Jesus. Don't take your desires too far and begin to worship them as your god, laying down all your time, energy, and relationships at the expense of other vital aspects of your life. This is a sin that "easily besets us" (Hebrews 12:1), no matter our walk of life or career calling.

When it comes down to it, no one—not your boss, your spouse, your parent, or anyone else—can tell you what you're passionate about. Only two people know your deepest passions: you and Jesus. Be on guard, because the Identity Thief will try to discourage you, deaden your heart, and make you believe lies. He will tell you, "You're not good enough," or "You don't have what that person has," or worse, "The Fiat 500 is enough for you." If you hear a whisper of doubt, know it comes from the most poisonous liar. The Identity Thief does not want you to discover or act on your passion because when you do, you are increasing your horsepower.

Remember this: knowing your passions is life changing. They are what will help you endure times of testing. Plugging in our strengths and unplugging our weaknesses is important, but passion speaks to the heart and prepares the body and soul for transformation. Transformation requires self-awareness of where you are now. Don't miss it. Feel the power of your passion as the engine revs—and leave the Fiat behind.

AN ILLUSTRATION TO REMEMBER: MY LAWN PASSION

Not all passions are purposeful passions. Let me illustrate. One day I was driving when on the radio I heard the hosts talking about crazy things people do. A caller started to tell the host that a friend of his is so looney about his lawn that before people leave a party at his house, he begins to rake the footprints his guests left behind. Funny, but this didn't sound abnormal to me. The caller went on to say, "Yeah. My friend Joe sure loves his lawn!"

Gasp! Could they have been speaking about me? As the caller kept talking, I realized, *I know that voice.* It was then it hit me: he was most definitely speaking about me.

I don't know about you, but when I leave this earth, I sure don't want people remembering me as the man who truly loved his lawn.

Now, I had a passion for my lawn, that's undeniable. As a matter of fact, I looked forward to the day each week when I would cut and trim it up, making it look like a park. I would put my headphones on and mow down each row so that when the job was done, I could go back inside the house and look out the kitchen window to see perfect lines. Truly a beautiful sight! (At least to me!)

But just because I gained pleasure from it, did it mean that this "lawn passion" was pointing to my purpose—and therefore, my purposeful passion? Nope! It was simply something I enjoyed.

Operating outside of your purposeful passion can yield success. I know a lot of people who do, and they're seemingly successful and contented individuals. But they are also the same people who are unfulfilled in that they're missing the opportunities God has put before them. Just because they feel a degree of contentment doesn't mean that they haven't inwardly settled. They're missing the convergence point—the place where strengths and passion meet that ultimately points to purpose.

They have settled for something good, maybe. But your passions aren't only about what's good; they're also about who you were created to be. You're a unique individual with a unique voice and point of view. When you align yourself with your creator to do things that he has made plain to us, committing to walk in his general will, then your specific viewpoint, strengths, and passions are used with God-ordained purpose. I often see people cutting off their nose to spite their face. They think that following a passion is taking the easy, selfish way out. But I'm telling you, take inventory of the good passions God has already placed in you just as you do your strengths and weaknesses, because God has placed them there for a purpose.

Make no mistake, passion is a powerful force. A force that needs to be identified and released. Don't settle for less!

FOUR

Question #4 – What Is Your Brand?

"Your brand is what other people say about you when you're not in the room."
— JEFF BEZOS, FOUNDER OF AMAZON

"A good name is more desirable than great riches; to be esteemed is better than silver or gold."
— PROVERBS 22:1

BRAND INTRODUCTION: BUILDING/IDENTIFYING YOUR BRAND

Progressive, Allstate, Geico, State Farm, and Liberty Mutual. What do they all have in common? Yes, they're all insurance companies, but more than that, they have established their brand. Each has done so by employing effective marketing techniques that highlight the main aspects of building a brand. Various results occurred—for example, catchy slogans, symbols, or icons; specific color combinations; a person or even an animal, such as a lizard. All personify the brand. They have successfully created something consumers can identify with.

Why is this important, you may ask? Customer loyalty. A brand evokes emotions—good, bad, or indifferent.

A good brand is built on its consistency, promotes positive emotional responses, and can deliver its message of identity clearly and concisely. Any successful brand will repeatedly reinforce what it is that best represents who they are; that is the *stance* they have taken. For instance, the stance State Farm has taken is to be "like a good neighbor." Walmart has taken the stance of offering the lowest price guarantee. When a person or company decides what they stand for, it's their name that is then put on the line, whether it's reputable or not.

If Walmart reneged on their stance, a customer wouldn't trust that specific brand. As they build on that foundation, it's their consistency that will drive their label. Fail too often, or don't hold up to your word, and you're labeled untrustworthy. Always win, and you'll be the one everyone wants.

A stance, your name, and being labeled are three critical aspects of any brand. Do you know your brand? When people hear your name or see your face, a brand is attached. Their response can be positive, negative, or indifferent. But is who they're seeing a true representative of what you believe about yourself? A brand builder/identifier must answer some crucial questions. Overall, there are three peripheral questions and two primary questions to ask.

Peripheral

- What do you *stand* for?
- How do people *label* you?
- What does your *name* convey?

Primary

- What are you known for?
- Why do people come to you?

Beginning with the peripheral questions and working our way up in importance, let's dissect each one and see how they individually are building blocks to the overall goal: building/identifying your brand.

QUESTION #1: WHAT DO YOU STAND FOR?

Life will push and shove us, and trust me, neither Flo, the Gecko, nor the "good neighbor" folks will cover all the damage. When we face challenging times such as a cancer diagnosis, filing bankruptcy, or losing a loved one, we need to have a consistent brand that people can lean on and trust. Taking a stance is a firm decision to consistently move in a specific direction no matter what comes your way. Some people have taken a stance to not be broken by the world and to stand firm in faith no matter the circumstances. Personally, I aspire for this and respect those who represent this stance well.

Really, there's no such thing as a listing of the "Top 5 Stances to Take." More so they are attitudes and beliefs one carries inside. For instance, have you heard of Harriet Tubman, the great Underground Railroad conductor? If a slave, mid-escape, ever tried to turn back, Harriet would pull a gun out and say to the person, "You will live free or die a slave."[1] Her stance was clear: "We are going for *it all,* or not going *at all.*" Her attitude was "we keep moving," and her belief was that where they were moving to was worth dying for. She took a stance and was immovable from that position.

Maintaining your stance is so important because this is how we inspire people. Now, if the person who claims they will never quit opens a business but then changes their mind after receiving their first bill, this gives them no ground to stand on with anyone who believed in them. Harriet did just the opposite, but more on her soon.

QUESTION #2: WHAT DOES YOUR NAME CONVEY?

When someone labels you as, say, a liar or as honest, what is it they're labeling? Are they saying, "Your satellite dish is a liar," or "Your back door is honest"? Nope! It is your name that is receiving such labels. For example, if a company promises next day-delivery, but it takes a month for you to get the product, you'll no doubt lose trust in that promise—and in the company. The feelings of distrust become thoughts about a company like "(Company name) are liars. They said I would get my product a month ago!"

My objective here is to challenge you to think about what people think when they see you, and more importantly, what they think when you leave, and *most* importantly, whether these opinions align with who you are at your core. The one thing that should capture who we are is our name. It identifies us and connects us to our individuality. There is power within your character; your name is the way others will recognize this character and label you. Your name is a massive part of your brand.

Your name is important, write it here: _____.

 "A person's name is to him or her the sweetest and most important sound in any language."[2]
— Dale Carnegie

QUESTION #3: HOW DO PEOPLE LABEL YOU?

Whether in the heat of battle or in the presence of peace, who you are should be the same. Squeeze an orange and what comes out? Orange juice, of course. We can identify a piece of fruit by the peel. In turn, we know what to expect when we squeeze it. Can you trust the orange to produce OJ? You can, because your history of squeezing oranges has always made orange juice, and whether you want orange juice or not, you can trust that the inside of the fruit matches the outside (the peel).

Every slave looked at Harriet Tubman in this way. Whether they wanted to risk their life or decided against escaping, they had to recognize what she had already accomplished. She had been through the trenches and fought through life-threatening situations, freeing many people.

When you're in a tight spot and getting squeezed, what comes out of you? Does your juice match the peel?

I always recommend being dedicated to being real, no matter what. Be consistent and dependable, no matter the circumstance. Others will notice your persistence in these areas of character. Establishing a reliable, authentic brand is a must for anyone with a mission to accomplish. If you don't carefully and purposefully build your label, others will gladly label you for themselves.

Just as there are three ways a person can perceive a brand (good, bad, indifferent), there are three labels a person can be labeled with.

1. **A genuine label.** This is when the person has been labeled accurately inside and out. It is genuinely who they are. Kind of like the orange.
2. **An ingenuine label.** This is when someone is labeled inaccurately. As the children's story goes, sometimes wolves put on a sheep's clothing. Other times lions can be so deceptively quiet that their unsuspecting target may be utterly unaware of the impending danger they face. Either way, bad or good, the label given to such people is inaccurate and ingenuine (and potentially harmful).
3. **An unidentifiable label.** This is when a person is either all over the place or indecisive. Both yield the same result: an unclear persona, character, and stance.

When looking to build your brand, make sure it is a genuine label —a title that has shown to be true. Referring to our heroine of this section once again, it didn't matter if the slave owners said, "This cursed woman is taking our slaves and leading them to the North to be free!" or whether a slave gladly said, "Harriet will lead us to our freedom in the North!" Both genuinely labeled her a liberator. Even though some hated what she did, they couldn't deny what she was doing.

That's the power of being the orange. From the peel to the juice, the fruit is so clearly what it is that no person in their right mind could possibly call it a banana or a coconut. If people aren't labeling you according to your core values, you might have some more proving to do, at least in their eyes.

Galatians 5:22–23 says, "But the fruit of the Spirit is love, joy, peace, patience, kindness, goodness, faithfulness, gentleness, self-control. Against such things, there is no law." We can learn a lot from what these verses are saying. All the qualities above are authentic, and therefore they can only produce good fruit. Nothing is more satisfying than biting into a nice juicy Florida orange; this is also true for the satisfaction of seeing who you are influence another person.

Just like with any business, different systems and procedures need to be mastered to produce success. A genuine label is just one of the systems that is required for success. The factory is your brand.

QUESTION #4: WHAT ARE YOU KNOWN FOR?

When others look at you, talk about you, or interact with you, you want them to see the totality of your brand. Do you know how your friends, family, and coworkers view you? What is their experience with you? What I'm really asking is, what are you known for? If you think you're labeled accurately across the board, keep at it. Continue through with consistency and let your brand grow. But if you think you've been mislabeled and are known for something that you're not proud of, you can do something about that.

There comes a time in all our lives when we ask, "Who am I?" Such an inquirer is in search of their purposeful identity. Their brand is imperative to discovering who they are. If you think you're known for the wrong things, you can still be a brand-changer.

I had a friend in high school who many saw as only a "brainy" kid. He was the kid the jocks would go to for answers on tests. Then in the span of one summer, he went from pumping out 100s on tests to pumping out 270-pound reps on the bench. He must have had enough of the whispering classmates claiming his strongest muscle was his brain, and for better or worse he chose to take a stance. New labels became linked to his name and voila—he became a brand-changer. Just like my friend, many people out there are redefining what it is they're known for.

I believe Harriet Tubman is the greatest brand-changer of all time. What is she known for? She freed dozens of slaves through the Underground Railroad, and so much more. Easily, I can see her eluding a chase, fighting for survival, and leading many lives to freedom. What a woman! She epitomizes the idea of what we mean by a "good brand." She's known in history as a fighter, a leader, a survivor, a dreamer, and an independent and heroic woman.

To her master, she was no more than a piece of property that could be exchanged for the right price, but she thought otherwise. As low as she was in social status, her true self emerged as a result of her courageous actions. Next time the plantation owners saw her, she would be genuinely labeled a free woman. I see her as being a great brand-changer for leading herself and dozens of others to liberty, which ultimately changed what they were known for.

If you are mislabeled, change is very much a possibility, but only if you're willing and intentional. Moving forward without thinking out your decisions can bring about the danger of your potentially closing this book and being no different from when you opened it. In the real world, we have ups and downs. It's the downs that reveal who we *truly* are—in other words, what we are known for.

QUESTION #5: WHY DO PEOPLE COME TO YOU?

Harriet was told dozens of times how worthless and foolish she was, but despite that, she knew her brand. As she received whippings and physical abuse from such a young age, it could have been easy for her to let go of any hope for change. Years passed, yet the beatings, which caused her bones to become frail, only created an iron will deep inside. When she bled, she was bleeding her brand; when crying, she was crying her brand. Part of that brand was refusing to be broken.

While I'm sure the Underground Railroad meant something wonderful to the people held in slavery, I can say confidently the name Harriet Tubman represented more to a slave than the words *Under-*

ground Railroad. Why? She didn't stop caring after obtaining her freedom. She escaped the life of slavery and dedicated her remaining years to helping others to liberty. But consider this: Why would dozens of slaves risk their lives and their family's lives, fleeing from the plantation, knowing that every dog and gun from the plantation would be ferociously chasing after them?

Moreover, why would they risk life, safety, and freedom, believing in a woman who barely measured five feet tall? It wasn't because of her height, or her eloquent pitch for a free life; it was her name. Her name was trustworthy. It brought comfort and assurance to the listener. Harriet Tubman conducted many escapes, and not one of the slaves she took under her wing ever failed to reach freedom. Think about that. Harriet never lost a slave under her supervision. Better than being the best at what she did, she was loyal too. No slave, as they were in the process of an escape, ever had to worry about her stopping in the middle of the journey to say, "Sorry, everybody. I'm throwing in the towel. Let's turn back."

No, Harriet wouldn't be broken. She wouldn't even allow her companions to jeopardize the chance at obtaining their freedom. She was not just the best, but she was also trustworthy and honest. The kind of person who could cause you to melt in your chair with excited anticipation or melt with anxiety on the trail with a gun pointed at you if you dared risk the escape effort by trying to turn back. If she walked into your slave quarters on the plantation, hope would overwhelm you as you knew your freedom was imminent.

Her name meant *everything* to the people. It was an excellent name to have on her side, and that's why they flocked to her by the dozens.

TOOL #8: 5 QUESTIONS TO IDENTIFY YOUR BRAND

As you just read, answering these five questions is critical to a whole, authentic, and powerful brand. Take a few minutes and answer these questions.

What do you stand for? _____

_____.

What does your name convey? _____

_____.

How do people label you? _____

_____.

What are you known for? _____

_____.

Why do people come to you? _____

_____.

BRANDING: NEEDING AFFIRMATION VS. NEEDING CHANGE

AFFIRMING A BRAND: THOMAS EDISON

What if someone labels you strictly by what they see, without knowing what it is you stand for? There are real-world factors that affect our brand, regardless of how we want people to perceive us. Sometimes the only way to change someone's mind is to show them they're wrong. But is this changing your brand or simply reaffirming what is already there?

Take Thomas Edison, who failed roughly a thousand times while trying to create a functioning lightbulb. The people who were close to him would have seen such repetitive failure, perhaps connecting his name to the label *wacky dreamer* or *constant disappointment*. He was an intelligent man, and this would help validate his sanity to a certain extent, but you can bet some people were actively tarnishing his name, such as the *New York Times*. Every time he failed, it gave his critics more fuel. After his five-hundredth attempt, he was already labeled a failure, and his good name was at the mercy of those who wanted nothing more than to see him fail. Yet Edison persevered and eventually did succeed. He is remembered as a genius and pioneer in the Industrial Age.

Edison needed to affirm his brand. His stance was that he was an inventor and not a failure. In fact, he said that the lightbulb was a thousand-step process, not a project that failed a thousand times. He took a stance, ignored what others said about his name, and focused on building what he knew could be done; he showed his critics that they were wrong and had mislabeled him.

The truth is that even though we are labeled, that doesn't mean the critics are right. Any builder of a brand must hold firm to the stance they take, build their label through consistent action, and be aware of what attitudes their name might be associated with—good or bad—and then work hard defending all the three aspects that together is their brand.

CHANGING A BRAND: MY PERSONAL STORY

Perhaps you're not Thomas Edison and have done some bad stuff in the past and are known for some pretty ugly things. That's okay. I believe you can be transformed. I've seen it done. If you have a haunting past, you can still be a brand-changer. By now you may have figured out that I'm not proud of some of the things I've done in the past.

People often sacrifice their unique brand in exchange for the world's brand. When I read about this, I think of what my name means. If someone in the world hears my name, what do they think? When Jesus hears my name, what does he think? I've always loved my name, but not everybody does or has. Some people have hated the name Joe Pellegrino. That's my fault. I used to be a swindler. I would cheat people and lie to get what I wanted; it didn't matter the cost. What did they think when they heard my name? "Oh no! Joe." My brand was a liar, thief, swindler, and con. I had plenty of character, but it was all bad.

I was once a slave to my negative and destructive ways. And then, like the slaves Harriet led to freedom, I was redirected to become identified with a completely different brand. I may not have had integrity back then, but God wasn't finished with me.

I don't care who you were when you opened this book. All I care about is who you're becoming while you read it—and who you'll be when you're done. Thanks be to God that I was tackled at the one-yard line when I was going the wrong way. Now I've taken the stance to do the same thing for others who need it. I can say, humbly and with confidence, that when I walk in the room, people say, "Oh yes! It's Joe." Not because I deserve it, but because I'm becoming the man who God created me to be. The "Oh yes!" part of it is just a byproduct of being obedient. My ego doesn't get big, but I know why I'm doing what I'm doing. I want to inspire people, improve their lives, and help them find their brand.

In this season of my life, I'm grateful to be able to say that others now see me as a life coach, Christian, entrepreneur, family man, and reliable person. I believe people know that I care for others and want to see them attain purpose and success in their lives. I'm willing to do what I can to help them achieve their goals. And seeing a guy like me turn from a life of dishonesty to a life of purpose shows others they can do it too. You see, others turn to me because I have persevered, I am consistent, and I have proven to be reliable. My brand is genuine and therefore has value.

 "A good name is more desirable than great riches; to be esteemed is better than silver or gold."
— Proverbs 22:1

FAKE BRANDS: ARE YOU REAL?

If you want change, great. Keep reading. If you're proud of your brand and not seeing a need for change, still keep reading. Perhaps you can help teach someone the importance of being the "real cheese." Let me explain.

A lot of people live life with no understanding that people are labeling them all day every day, and that they are passing some sort of judgment on their brand. The best thing that can happen is for a person to receive a brand (or name) that reflects precisely who they are at their core. For example, if you genuinely care about others, it's significant that others see that you genuinely care through, say, acts of significant or even sacrificial kindness. Then you become labeled as a kind man or woman, and this in turn reflects who you are at your core and becomes your brand.

The opposite is also true as it relates to a person building their brand. When you're branded in a way that doesn't reflect who you truly are—perhaps due to inconsistencies in your character or passively accepting who others say you are, or simply being unsure about how to release your core values into the world—this type of labeling becomes detrimental to your purposeful identity. This holds true, whether the negative branding is self-imposed or has been imposed on you by others.

In fact, living a life to please others or a life that is defined by others isn't a life with purposeful identity at all. Instead, it's living life as a "character"—a distorted misrepresentation of who you were truly designed to be. The Identity Thief knows this all too well. We can constantly find ourselves amid a battle to compromise—to please the people around us, even if it is contrary to what we believe or who we are. Doing this affects our brand. Continuing to pursue a brand that doesn't reflect our core identity is spiritually, mentally, and physically draining.

Picture it like this: Say you work at major theme park and your job is to impersonate a famous character. The job requires you come to work full of energy and unequivocally ready to play the part of a specific character. Your voice, movements, dress, and every other piece of you must reflect this character. Now like any other job, imagine you had to do this all day every day without a break or day off. You go to work and are demanded, by the expectations of others, to play that character. You go out to dinner and have to play that character. Go home and have to play that character. Wake up and do it again. Eventually you will run out of energy "pretending."

If you're someone who has been pretending and perhaps are exhausted, it may be time to get intentional about changing your brand. This can be tricky, though, because there are many temptations from the Identity Thief, who wants you to please the masses, become a number in the crowd, and lose your unique identity. Fear of judgment often drives us to create this false reality, one in which we brand ourselves as an acceptable character, contrary to our genuine label. For example, perhaps we don't agree with lying but don't call out our chronically lying boss. Not saying anything would lead that boss to believe you are okay with their dishonesty. That needs to change. Don't play the character; be you and stand firm in that.

The truth is we are continually changing, every day, every year. The change I'm referring to is the kind of change that either builds on a purposeful identity or tears it down. Living just to please the world is not a practice that brings about good change. People who dress to blend in with a popular opinion are sacrificing their inner brand and unique identity in the process. Go in their closets and you will see a wardrobe of counterfeit clothes. Go deep into their heart and you will see their true self enslaved to the world, secretly longing to be free.

There's a scene in a recent movie where the main character is unhappy at work, friendless, lost in the world, and on the verge of depression.[3] The young man comes to the end of a long day and hops in bed alone. You can see the sadness and loneliness on his face. Before he turns in, he snags his phone, turns to the window, and says, "Okay! Let's give them what they want!" He takes a picture of Los Angeles, crops in a full moon, and writes, *Wow! I'm so grateful for my city. My amazing job. And all my amazing friends.* He then posts it on social media.

You can see the façade as plain as day. The juice doesn't match the peel here. And the whole let's give "them" what they want? The "them" represents the demands of the world.

Many people are worried about how others view them, so much so that they compromise their character and integrity to create that "perfect" brand. In reality, what they're doing is becoming one of the crowd, blending in and losing themselves. They give anything to flow with the current and avoid the upstream battle, no matter the cost, even if throwing their arms up and falling face first in society's river is what it takes.

Beware of the seductions of society, because they will tear apart an unguarded identity. Jesus has given every person an authentic, invaluable brand at their core. Once we know who we are in him, the goal is for our outer self to be a mirror image of our inner self. Harriet Tubman was set free on the inside long before escaping slavery. Her mission was for her outside to be a mirror reflection of what lay within. So, if a genuine label is when our outside character reveals our true inner self, the opposite is valid for an ingenuine label, in which a false outside veil hides our inner character. Here's an example of an ingenuine label.

Once upon a time, Velveeta was made from real cheese. But in a rapidly growing industry—the dairy industry—in order to keep up, not only did branding have to grow and change, but so did the product. Driven by the fear of being left behind, Kraft had to find a way to create a product that would be able to flow with the demand of the people. Soon there was no more real cheese in Velveeta.

What did the executives do to suppress this truth? They advertised their product as Liquid Gold. Not Liquid Cheese. Liquid Gold. For most people, they just need to know—or rather believe—a product is "liquid gold" and they will buy in. Here's the truth: In the process of becoming a cheese substitute (fake cheese), Velveeta's flavor became milder so more people would be likely to enjoy it. It went from a product containing cheese to a cheese substitute, and they labeled it as gold. Some might see how that's an ingenuine label.

Isn't that ironic? The more Velveeta became fake and mild, the more people bought in—kind of like the guy who made the fake post. So many people these days are similarly branding themselves like Velveeta: Appease the masses. Really, what's happening is a loss of self. The Identity Thief is at work, continually trying to get us to fall into accepting this loss of self. Remember, he doesn't want you to find your purposeful identity. What he promotes is worldly wisdom. People believe that creating flashy and bright brands, whether they're honest or dishonest, is what branding is all about—just so long as they will attract new customers. Viewing branding this way is superficial and greedy, yet if it makes money, this is wisdom to them, at least according to the world's standard.

"The wisdom of this world is foolishness in God's sight; as it is written, 'He catches the wise in their craftiness.'"
— 1 Corinthians 3:19

He catches them in their craftiness, or should I let my inner dad out and say he catches them in their *Kraftiness* (Kraft is the maker of Velveeta). Not that I have anything against the brand. They have good mac and *cheese*; it's just what Kraft did was take real cheese, transformed it into fake cheese, and then advertised it as a desirable product, one of good quality. God sees that type of deception as foolishness. The outside says *Liquid Gold*, but there's no trace of any real cheese on the inside. Imagine if real aged cheese and processed fake cheese cost the same price. Which would you buy?

Harriet Tubman was the real cheese all along. Her master saw her as a small, ignorant, and worthless woman. She was a totally mislabeled person, compared to who she truly was. Kraft and the guy from the movie perpetrated a deceptive image, which is utter foolishness according to God. With Harriet, what people saw was what they got. She fought for the real picture: her genuine label. When someone's outward brand matches what's on the inside, that is a genuine label.

I challenge you to ask yourself how much real cheese is in your brand. And then ask if that's what you're known for. If not, fight to exemplify the real cheese. Don't give in and be known as "Liquid Gold"—just a cheese substitute.

ARE YOU LIVING HONESTLY?

Transparency is a character trait of honesty. Hopefully, if you're reading this book, you want to be honest, and the best place to start is with yourself. Are you tried and true? Dependable, trustworthy, credible, consistent, and loyal? It's essential to know these qualities so you can build on or change your brand.

Have you ever met someone who's trying so hard to be someone they aren't? You know, the guy who couldn't play football even if his life depended on it—and yet he idolizes Tom Brady. Dresses like him, tries to talk like him, and even begins to pick up his hobbies. Eventually, he gets branded as a mini Tom Brady by his bar buddies—the butt of a sad joke. He's not genuine or authentic; he's merely an imposter, pretending to be someone he's not.

While it's true that learning from others is essential, and anyone can learn something from Tom about throwing, there's still a big difference between learning from a person and trying to be what you believe that person represents or wants. When you need advice or mentoring, whom do you turn to? Why? What is it about that person that draws you to them? Most often, these people have built up and defined their brand. They are dependable, trustworthy, and deliver, a person Tom Brady has proven to be time and time again.

Whether you're idolizing a person or becoming one of the crowd, you're doing the same thing: abandoning your unique, God-given brand. Millions of people are fakers, following the masses and trends but never going where they're destined to be. You don't find oranges on apple trees, nor do you find wolves trying to pass themselves off as lions. How ridiculous! The orange has its place, as does the apple, the lion, and the wolf. Even if an orange could try to pretend to be an apple, sooner or later, when someone picked a basket that was supposed to contain apples, they would be shocked (and not happy) to find something quite different from what they expected.

Live honestly. Be you. God didn't create you to be a Tom Brady. He created you to be unique. One of a kind. To have your own brand. So, what are *you* known for?

TOOL #9: THE NOW AND SOON

When a Canadian hears the name Terry Fox, they think *fighter*. When an Australian hears the name Nick Vujicic, they think *leader*. And when an American hears the name Harriet Tubman, they think *liberator*. These labels are one of many you could give them, but they are genuine, nonetheless. Their juice matched the peel. But each had to decide, in the *now* of their lives, whether they would rise or fall. In other words, take a stand.

The *now* is what some might call fate, luck, or even the chance of a lifetime. But I will say it's much more than any of those. It's a defining moment that can determine what our brand becomes. We usually face these moments of decision in tough times. Terry's was in the wake of his surgery; Nick's came just minutes away from suicide; and Harriet's came after years of beatings and oppression, when she saw her chance to run. Each faced a moment when they could fight to rise up to the next level or forfeit the opportunities afforded them, acting out of a sense of despair. What drove their decision was a vision of the *soon*. *Soon* Terry would run, *soon* Nick would preach, *soon* Harriet would be a free woman. They saw it on the inside, before they actually experienced it in their circumstances. This is vision!

Let's take some time to build self-awareness. What are you currently known for? Write it below. Then write what you would like to be known for (a vision for the future).

Known for Now

1. _____.
2. _____.
3. _____.
4. _____.
5. _____.

What You Will Soon Be Known For

1. _____.
2. _____.
3. _____.
4. _____.
5. _____.

Think back to your passions and strengths that can help make these traits become a reality. Remember, a decision is required, and it must be intentional.

So, what are you known for? What would others say about you behind closed doors? How have you reacted or responded to the trials of life? Are you an overcomer? Here are some things I would like to be known for, and maybe you would too:

- A leader who challenges people and helps them achieve their goals
- A parent who encourages and equips their family for generations to come
- A person who is supportive, empathetic, and reliable to others
- A person who creates an environment where people feel safe and comfortable to be themselves
- An innovator who is always trying to make a difference in the community

These are just some ideas to get the mental juices flowing and help you visualize what a brand might be.

AN ILLUSTRATION TO REMEMBER: CLEAN YOUR ATTIC

If your brand isn't where you know it should be, it's time to right the ship. When you're gone, the brand you've spent a lifetime building up is what you leave behind. Then it becomes your legacy.

There was something that took place not long ago that could have easily put my name in jeopardy. Four years ago, on a beautiful November day, my wife was urging me to clean out the attic. I didn't want to tackle that project, but now and then it's good to go through the old stuff. So, I crawled up and down, piling all the boxes in our driveway. Memories began flooding my mind. My collection of baseball magazines, old college textbooks, and a bunch of the little things that make life so worth it. It was cool to see it all again after such a long time.

I always said the baseball collection was my "million-dollar" collection. It was refreshing seeing the magazines again after not bothering with them for so long. Felt good living in the past, until the past seemingly tried to bite me. Something else was in my baseball collection. Something that didn't belong in my house anymore. All I could think was, *What is that doing here?*

The process of separating the good from the ugly within the boxes would have been risking putting myself back into a place that once consumed me, one that was killing me at the time. Instead, I simply decided that the magazines had to go. I backed my car up and loaded all the boxes in and brought everything to the dump.

That was truly a hard thing to do. That baseball collection was filled with gems from the 1970s through that day. My brand may have been the frat guy who loved frat things once upon a time, but that wasn't my brand anymore; I had changed it. I wasn't about to allow all the years of growth and development to be for nothing. I could tell my boys about my past, which I have, but something changes when you see it up close and personal. For myself, leaving a Christ-centered legacy is not just a mission—it's my life.

I realized that day, my house's attic wasn't the only attic that was getting cleaned. There was one last piece of my heart that had to be freed. For me, the healing took place as I threw away a small piece of the past while giving up my baseball collection, which had once been a big piece of me. It was a sacrifice that was well worth the effort to preserve what the Lord and I have worked to build: my true identity, which is an authentic, trustworthy, and honest brand.

FIVE

Question #5 - What Do You Believe?

"If you don't stand for something, you will fall for anything."
— GORDON A. EADIE

"All I have seen teaches me to trust the Creator for all I have not seen."
— RALPH WALDO EMERSON

"To believe in something, and not to live it, is dishonest."
— MAHATMA GANDHI

INTRO: WHAT DO YOU BELIEVE?

Michelangelo said, "The sculpture is already complete within the marble block before I start my work. It is already there; I just have to chisel away the superfluous material."[1] What he was saying is that the masterpiece that is to be is already in you. God completed your sculpture long ago.

The last four chapters have been a tool to help you to either chip away at the excess material in your life or discover the best pieces of who you are. Now we've reached a key component: What do you believe? Our beliefs can come from many different sources, but a few examples of those might include our own experiences, popular opinion, and society. Each of them is powerful and can influence every aspect of our life. Whether or not we take that job, who we decide to have a relationship with, and the dreams we choose to pursue are all influenced by our belief system.

Beliefs, when seen in this light, will ultimately shape who you are. Yes, they shape the sculpture of you. Here's the problem: most of us failed art class. I couldn't sculpt a square, let alone come anywhere near the majesty captured in the *Pieta* by Michelangelo. To say it more plainly, we genuinely are unique sculptures, but that doesn't mean we should be the ones holding the chisel. Yet most of us are doing that very thing, because down deep inside, being in control is the best thing for our own lives, or so we believe. Some people are not only holding the chisel, but are also grasping it with a death grip. I believe we don't need to be in charge. Do you believe that? To put it differently, can you *truly* be the captain of your own fate?

Believe it or not, our vision for our own life is usually incomplete, and, even worse, is often impaired. We're like a person who has been blinded and bound in chains. Sometimes that limited vision can be likened to a person who has grown far too comfortable with the dull, boring routines of everyday life. Such unfortunate folks are generally headed in the wrong direction—or even headed nowhere at all. These vision impairments are threats to the pursuit of finding a purposeful identity. Whenever we believe that we're the Master Sculptor, our lives are exposed to such risks. I used to think I was capable of being in charge, but in time came to realize that I'm not. I found out that I had to give up the chisel. I then learned that when you pass the chisel to the Master, three main revelations come in a person's life (among other possible ones):

1. The blind receive sight.
2. The enslaved gain their liberty.
3. We learn the right way.

As a result of the ongoing sculpting process, these three revelations have become apparent. You don't have to believe what I'm saying, although I have personally experienced them and do believe them for myself. I've also seen hundreds of others experience them. Just as important as believing in something is testing those beliefs.

FOUR BLIND MEN

So, what do you believe? Are you a Democrat or a Republican? Do you believe in a healthy diet or self-indulgence? Do you believe in changing the world, or are you content with current circumstances? Do you believe in God? Do you believe in *you*? It's essential to know these things because they shape who you are. The fact that our beliefs shape us is evidenced in everything from larger issues such as politics, down to very personal items such as our favorite foods.

The wide-range availability of different belief systems often results in those beliefs being tested or challenged in some way. The Republican debates the Democrat, the youth challenges the elder about rules (or the elders scold the children for their tastes in music), and the list goes on. What I've found is that true beliefs stand the difficult tests that will inevitably come, be they from society, a teacher, or a neighbor.

People are frequently in the process of adopting beliefs that they think will fulfill them. Seeking this fulfillment is natural because, as I stated previously in the chapter on weakness, God has given us the inclination to fill in the empty spaces in our life. Still, however, belief-grafting is often the preferred answer for those who have inner holes in their life, especially when they want an immediate filling.

Belief-grafting is a term I define as the fusing of another's beliefs or set of ideas into a person's life without testing those beliefs or previously considering such views. Pretty much, they hear and say, "Oh, wow. That sounds good. I'll live that way," only to give up on it not long afterward, or find out that they just entered a cult of some kind (and that is another story entirely). Accepting false or unclear beliefs is detrimental to our identity and can pull us away from our destiny. It's kind of like seeing something only in part.

For instance, four blind men walk up to an elephant and begin feeling different parts of the animal. One feels the trunk, another the leg, another the tail, and finally, one feels the ear. After that, each one of them describes the shape of the elephant. Their descriptions were all different, and none were able to describe the animal accurately because each man only got a piece of the story, rendering their individual vision for the elephant incomplete.

People do this in real life as well. They take a belief and don't fully unpack it. It's vital to search for truth and ask why you believe what you do. Do some unpacking, feel around, and see if there's truth to what you believe or if you're just belief-grafting someone else's belief system. Ask some questions. As the apostle Paul said, "Do not treat prophecies with contempt but test them all; hold on to what is good, reject every kind of evil" (1 Thessalonians 5:20–22).

Ask questions and put what God says about you to the test: Why am I built this way? Why do I have these particular strengths, weaknesses, passions? Why do I believe what I believe? What is happening in the world around me, and how should I interact with it? A lot of people won't ask themselves these questions because they're afraid of what they might find. The irony with the four blind men is that they stopped searching after discovering what they thought was the answer. None of them asked each other about it, and that's why their descriptions were all different and incomplete.

I have found that the truth is bigger than the proverbial elephant. In addition, I've discovered that asking a question not only helps paint the entire image of the elephant, but that questions are key to guiding us in the process of building a strong foundation for our beliefs.

If you've answered the previous four questions, please don't stop there. Now is the time to discover your foundation. As you search, do it with a humble heart, because seeking to prove people wrong often leads to someone getting hurt. Test what people are saying and see if there's any truth to it. Most importantly, test what God says about you and see what truth comes to light.

The first revelation is now complete on how the blind receive sight. An incredibly wise man said, "Ask, and you will receive" (Matthew 7:7 CEV).

THE EAGLE ON THE ELEPHANT

The more questions you ask, the more answers you'll get. Not every answer is complete or accurate, yet this shouldn't hinder you from asking. When you discover who you are, you kill who you aren't, and it all starts with the foundation, which is knowing who you are and why you're here. By default, the reverse is true as well: when you give life to who you're not, you kill (or paralyze) who you are.

A purposeful identity demands a sound understanding of the nature of your life's purpose. Having a heart of discernment between truth and lies is also imperative to finding your purposeful identity. The day you find these answers is liberating, kind of like the day an eagle flies for the first time. To illustrate the importance of the eagle's ability to fly, let's think about a fledgling.

A lost fledgling, misplaced and confused, meandered aimlessly about in the wild Serengeti. Alone and worried, the fledgling asked somebody where he was meant to be. The person he asked was one of the blind men. The blind man listened and could immediately tell that a bird was posing the question. He was also able to hear birds that were perched on top of the elephant, so he told the fledgling that he should join up with his fellow birds, naturally. (Jesus said if the blind lead the blind, they will both end up in a ditch, as you may recall.)

Although unsure at first, the fledgling conceded. After all, the birds did look like him and seemed to enjoy being on the elephant's back. The fledgling climbed up and made a place for himself among new friends. The other birds told him a little about themselves: they were oxpeckers, a native African bird that eats the ticks, parasites, and other bugs that live on the elephant for food, and in turn, get a free ride by doing so.

At first, the fledgling didn't like the taste of bugs, but in time, he adjusted to the flavor. It also took some time to make friends with his fellow birds, but it seemed like they never stayed in one place. The oxpeckers spent almost half of their adult life sitting on animals, but they bounced from elephant to elephant, never hanging around in one place too long. The fledgling couldn't fly like the others and was seemingly bound to this one elephant. How sad.

Unable to go with his friends when they flew from their host, he began to feel trapped. He didn't think he had anyone to share his burden. Something just wasn't right. He felt more lost than when he had initially climbed up on the elephant's big back.

As time went on and the fledgling grew, he noticed that he was different from the other birds, given his large talons, body, and beak. He thought back to the day when the blind man led him to the elephant. The fledgling was still without answers concerning his deep and perplexing questions about who he was and where he was meant to be. The oxpeckers couldn't give him the answers he yearned for, not necessarily because they didn't know who he was, but simply because the fledgling was afraid to ask.

Without identity, and afraid to seek guidance, our now-growing fledgling reluctantly accepted the idea that the blind man's original direction must have been right all along. He came to embrace the notion that he would live on the elephant for the rest of his life. His feelings of depression, which had gradually crept into his life, now intensified and stomped on his feathers, or so it felt to the poor fledgling. The only thing that seemed to keep him going was the occasional sighting of a distant speck in the sky. He didn't know why, but he wondered what could soar across the sky as elegantly as that tiny black speck.

As days continued to melt by in the unforgiving Serengeti heat, the fledging moved farther from the sights and sounds of his environment, other than the dull sound of his own sad and listless voice. Things were tough for the confused bird; he often wondered why his life seemed to be so disconnected and unfulfilled compared to that of the oxpeckers. He stopped seeking typical connections with friends. Observing their continual happiness only made him feel worse. At the end of each day's journey, he longingly watched the faint black speck in the sky. He had no understanding that the reason the oxpeckers lived a fulfilled life but he didn't was because each bird has a different purpose. If only that simple yet profound discovery would occur to him, hope would be restored.

This place in the story is a critical moment in the fledgling's life. And that can apply to us too, because we have *all* done what he did, at one time or another: indulged in self-pity, compared our lives to those around us, not followed our true hearts, etc. These are always dangerous things to do. Most often, we get this hopeless feeling that the life we seek is unattainable, and this belief takes away hope rather than supplies it. Hope comes in a much different way. Now back to the story.

Just as all seemed lost, the fledgling heard a screech from above that made his heart throb. Although loud and piercing, it wasn't frightening at all; instead, the call caused the fledgling's feathers to quiver with delight. It was as if he received an invitation to be free. For the first time in weeks, he felt something—something that seemed to banish all the sadness and loneliness he was experiencing. He smiled inwardly and then walked eagerly toward the tail of the elephant to position himself closer to the direction of the call.

The fledgling couldn't explain why, but all he wanted to do was leap into the air and find out who had made such a sound. He was intrigued, excited, and nervous all at once! Despite the intimidating distance that would need to be covered to gain his answer to this mystery, he still felt an intense desire to search the vast skies for the one whose sound seemed to be calling him. Put simply, he was experiencing the desire to fly. What a moment of discovery!

The other birds told him that flying's only purpose was to get from one elephant to the other, and up until this point, he hadn't been able to do it. Now, upon hearing a single call, he felt different. Suddenly, it was as if all he was purposed to do was fly. He asked, "Why am I built this way? Why do I have these strengths [talons, beak, body], these weaknesses, and these passions I now feel? Why do I believe what I believe?"

All of a sudden, the oxpeckers returned and warned him somewhat sternly (knowing that he had tried flying before and failed) to get away from the tail, that he could fall and be hurt by the elephant. Initially, he drew back. Again, the bird in the sky sent out a heart-throbbing screech. The intense desire returned to his heart. As an irresistible wind blew by, he spread his wings, and as natural as the wind itself, he took to the air. Once up, the truth became apparent. He climbed higher and higher in the open skies. His fledgling heart fairly raced with joy!

None of the oxpeckers flew as high as he did, but he could now see that there was more to flying than just alighting from elephant to elephant. In fact, the higher he went, the more satisfied he was. What a discovery! The questions he was once afraid to ask now had answers and had even become pillars to his new identity. He flew so high that he met the screeching bird. Instantly he knew he was home—where he was originally designed to be—flying free in the beautiful open skies.

The fledgling in this story, no doubt, reminds us of the potential in our lives. It also illustrates the importance of testing what we believe. When we test something out in good faith and arrive at accurate answers, these ideas then become the very foundations to our beliefs. So long as we don't ask, these foundational pillars won't exist—at least, not for us. Believe that you are flightless, misplaced, and ultimately hopeless, and your life will certainly mirror such beliefs. They will shape who you are.

But if you believe you're crafted for a purpose, that you're unique, and that you have an array of strengths at your disposal, again, your life will consistently mirror these beliefs. Even though the fledgling wasn't raised in ideal circumstances (by wise, loving guardians) and was led in the wrong direction by the blind person, neither experience could alter his God-given ability to fly.

The two key factors that determine when a bird starts to fly are timing and the willingness to jump. The day the fledgling flies is the day it becomes an eagle, which is also the same day his identity begins building and his life is changed. Another revelation is obtained: the discovery and exercise of purpose. This is also how the enslaved gain their liberty.

. . .

THE SEA CAPTAIN AND THE SEA

By now, you've surely experienced that life is much more than enjoying a perfect day on the beach. Even with the sun shining, a refreshing breeze blowing, and lazy waves barely touching the ends of our toes as they creep up on shore, we all recognize something as we stare out at the immense sea: the ocean is a mighty power that must be respected. Any deep-sea fisherman can tell you that the sea is much more than a lovely vacation destination. The sea is, after all, where the earth's wildest storms occur.

To some degree, we're all sea captains navigating the various oceans of life. Our direction is set by our belief systems (standard navigation system). Our belief systems tell each of us where to go and what route to take. Some even have a radar fix on which people to avoid and which ones to gravitate toward. Daily we set sail and depend on our beliefs to navigate us through the sea. Our beliefs are the foundation of our lives.

If the beliefs we live by are both the foundation and navigation systems of our life, then how do they help us when it comes to handling life's inevitable storms? The truth is that our beliefs are what tells the sea captain within us to hunker down confidently and ride out a storm, or to hastily flee as a storm approaches. Our beliefs are what keep us steady or cause us to sink when the storm hits, and they are what remain after the storm has passed.

So what happens when a sea captain out on the ocean is hit by a devastating storm? His beliefs were washed away, and now he's lost at sea with no direction. Now what?

When our foundations get shaken by an unexpected and unwelcome turn of events, so much so that it seems like all we can do is hold on (lest we crumble inwardly), what can we do? At those times, we must cling to our beliefs. The young captain who just got done watching his cargo fly overboard went through a life-changing event; his views went through difficult testing. Strong beliefs, tried beliefs, and true beliefs only become stronger in the aftermath of a storm, whereas weak beliefs, superficial beliefs, and untested beliefs get washed away by the angry, frightening waves, leaving a person more lost than when the storm first hit.

Jesus said this about storms and our foundation: "The rain came down, the streams rose, and the winds blew and beat against that house; yet it did not fall, because it had its foundation on the rock. But everyone who hears these words of mine and does not put them into practice is like a foolish man who built his house on sand. The rain came down, the streams rose, and the winds blew and beat against that house, and it fell with a great crash" (Matthew 7:25–27).

The good thing about when false or untested beliefs get washed away is that nothing is left, which provides room for building of a solid foundation. In the verses above, Jesus says something fundamental: "Everyone who hears these words of mine." When you apply these words in context with the passage, you can get the sense that he is watching over our lives and leading us in the way that builds a solid and firm house.

So, let me answer the question posed by the sailor lost at sea, "Now what?" Now is the time to build new beliefs—ones that will stand the test of the storms of life, ones that won't wash away. Now is the time to start on the only foundation that guarantees such security. Now is the time to get back on track. True beliefs always lead us the right way in life.

Like the sailor, we must be relentless when it comes to defining and discovering our beliefs. Once our beliefs form, they should be tested, defended, and protected. The Identity Thief is on the prowl, and he is going to do all he can to taint our beliefs. He is like the falling rain, the rising stream, and the blowing wind. He will instill fear into our heart so we doubt our faith and question our beliefs. But beliefs that undergo testing and hold up result in edification. When we get to this point, regardless of the Identity Thief's attempts to drown us, every drop of rain, all the pressure from the stream, and the swaying with the wind will only wash away superfluous material.

Now, to reveal the third revelation: how true beliefs lead us the right way in life.

. . .

A THOUGHT ON BELIEFS: BELIEFS DO SHAPE YOU

 "Just when the caterpillar thought the world was over it became a butterfly."
— Unknown

Every sculpture begins with a block of marble. I chose my block, a perfect rectangular slab dug out from deep within the earth. The piece of stone was beautiful, and I couldn't wait to get my hands on it and begin carving out the man I eagerly dreamed of being. I was going to become a self-made millionaire, a dad, and a baseball player—all the big dreams my mind could ponder. Every vision for my life revolved around one thing—me.

When I took control of the chisel, I learned the hard way that carving my statue was not going to be as easy as I thought. I had overlooked real vision, practice, patience, technique, skill, and development. On top of these, the slightest hiccup in my agenda threw my world upside down. It was like I was a sculptor trying to work during a massive earthquake. Things weren't working out, and slowly but surely I was ruining the perfect block of marble.

Then it hit me: I was running out of rock! I learned the hard way that I was playing a game with someone called the Identity Thief. I realized he wanted me to chisel that stone down to nothing. He wanted me lost, alone, and fragile, so he could come in and take what didn't belong to him—my life. I was in a fight with a fierce competitor with little knowledge of how I could get myself out of it. Broken and in need of repair, I had no choice but to pass God the chisel.

It wasn't long before things began to change. Whether it's how we see our kids or the lessons we learn in life, when divine insights flow from God into our life, we will see differently. I began to see lessons everywhere, in every corner of my surroundings. The little things that once quaked my life and knocked me down were now small steps that eventually led me to the right floor. Challenges didn't destroy my mood, and I began to move forward through every trial.

My life didn't become simpler (or easier) after passing God the chisel—there were many challenging and difficult times—but now, when the earthquake shook my world, I no longer tried to stop the tremors. Instead, I would ask God to do so, and he always has and still does. I am so grateful! And then I realized that the tremors were simply tools in the Master's hand to bring about something new and wonderful. I was being molded, shaped, and transformed into a statue I couldn't dream of sculpting on my own.

Have you ever put your beliefs to the test? Or do you believe something someone is saying without testing it at all? I didn't want to trust Jesus Christ because I like driving the boat, and that would mean giving up the helm and giving control to Him. So when my uncle gave me a Bible, all I wanted to do was prove it wrong. Yet all I could do was prove it right. It took several years to build me up to the man I am today. What was needed was a bit of chiseling from the Master Sculptor.

In my younger years, I was sculpting a kingdom for myself, living a life focused on fulfilling my wants. I wasn't concerned about God's kingdom at all. I believed being a frat boy was the answer, and from my slab of rock I chiseled a frat boy. I believed lying was the answer and chiseled a liar. I was a sculptor and believed I was the giant bird on the block.

But one day, I saw an eagle that was sculpted by the Master Sculptor. What I had carved was a life that was shallow, frail, and ignorant of what an authentic piece of art was. I was like one of the blind men who thought he had a rather good conception of what art looked like, but in reality, I absolutely did not. I was like a fragile sculpture that was just a storm away from shattering to a million pieces and being lost at sea. I was not a sculptor at all; instead, I was destroying my marble block.

Once I came to the bitter realization that I wasn't who I thought I was, the only answer was to go to the Master Sculptor. I asked, "What must I do to become better?" He told me to give him the chisel and then to trust Him. Believing in Him transformed me from being a worthless piece of stone to a redeemed and priceless work of art in His eyes.

"Your beliefs about yourself or the world around you can limit or unleash your purpose. The choice is yours."
— Joe Pellegrino

FINAL ILLUSTRATION TO REMEMBER: THE IDENTITY THIEF

Remember the television from chapter 1? I hope so.

One day, gazing upon his son from a distance, a father decided he would do something extraordinary for his child. Even though his son was rebellious, angry, and lost, the father's heart was compassionate and unchanging. The father saw his son struggling, so he continued with his plan. After the last piece was set in place, the father stepped back to look at his masterpiece. The work of art seemingly glowed before his very eyes. He just knew his son would love it.

The father went to his friends and told them what he planned to do. He was going to give away the house to his son, but not only that; he was also going to leave him enough money to pay the living expenses as well. His son would be set for life—free house and the money to pay to live there—and he would give it all and expect nothing but love in return. The father was giddy. He loved thinking of the look that would be on his son's face when he received the house.

Many pleaded with the father not to waste his time or resources, that his son was a lost cause and going to take the money and run. Well, the father knew his son loved him and believed that this was the best way to restore their relationship, so he went and searched for his son and, after finding him, brought him to the home. He explained, "Everything you see is now yours," and told him it was free of charge. The elegant rooms, the perfect architecture, beautiful kitchen, hand-carved floors, the full window overseeing the town—everything was meticulously thought out, prepared, and, amazingly, now given away for free.

The father's hand fell onto his son's shoulder. He gazed at his boy, but as the loving father's hand was brushed away, so was the expectation that his son would be grateful. His son's eyes were glued to the money. "This is mine?" the boy said, holding the stack of cash.

"Yes," the father said. But before he had even a moment to explain that it was for the living expenses, the door slammed rudely in his face, and his son was gone. He took the money and ran, leaving his intended home. Some might say the second that the greedy young man saw the cash, everything else was of no importance, even his love for his father. He was in search of something, and he believed the money would lead him to it.

The son traveled all over the town, searching in vain for this "something." He went from one end of the city to the other and found nothing but loneliness. A person who knew the father's plan had also figured the boy would take the money and run, and he saw this as a perfect opportunity to take advantage of the young and arrogant boy.

As the loneliness began to set in, the son remembered his father and the house. He turned around to head home, but he was unaware that he was being followed, and ran right into a big man, the biggest man he'd ever seen. He was tall, brawny, and menacing, but his cunning smile and smooth talk put the boy at ease. They fell into conversation, and the boy opened his heart to the seemingly understanding man. The man promised that the boy would find what he was searching for if he followed him.

The son believed this mystery man and followed his lead. Unbeknownst to him, this man had seen hundreds of other children lost and searching, and he knew just what to say to get them to trust him. He was a thief, a liar, and a manipulator—a complete con man, the full package.

The two went back into the town. The mystery man told the son that the city was overflowing with fulfilling opportunities, that all he had to do was live large, carefree, and rule-free to see them. The son liked the sound of that and once again believed what the mystery man was saying. They met many of the man's friends, who, for a few dollars, gave some life-changing "advice." The mystery man and the son bought fashionable clothes, ate the best food there was, and indulged themselves in everything the town had to offer. They even went to the carnival and played every game available. The con man was stealing cash right from the hand of the unwitting boy, all the while making him feel as if he had more money than he actually did.

The son was living it up without care, and trusted completely in the very experienced con. He flaunted his wealth, exploited those who served him, and loved the favor he received from the man's friends. It seemed that he had become a member of the mystery man's family. In the heat of his new life, he had forgotten entirely about what he went into the town to search for—purpose, identity, and love. Just as he felt himself about to rise another level on the mystery man's social ladder, perhaps becoming something exalted like a king, he painfully realized that all his money was gone. He was completely broke.

Unsure of what to do, the son turned to look in desperation for the mystery man, but he was gone. The foolish young man found himself entirely alone on the dark streets. All the man's friends shut their doors on the boy when he asked for help. He was out of cash, and they were out of advice. It all became real in a moment. He realized that he was lost, broke, and alone. He was devastated!

He became hungry, and with winter coming in, cold. Day after day, the air bit at the son's ears and spirit. He couldn't take it anymore and was on the verge of collapse. Then he remembered the house that his father built. The son searched for anyone who might be able to give him directions. He found a few people (some of his fathers' friends) who were happy to guide him the right way. While his son went out and ventured recklessly into the world, the father had made sure that the son's house was kept clean, warm, and stocked full of food. The bed was perfectly made, all ready for his return. The house had everything it needed, but the father couldn't help but go and get one last special gift.

The son returned to the house. To his surprise, it had been maintained and didn't lack anything. Enchanted by a sentimental warmth reminding him of peaceful days, the son felt a lump form in his throat. How could he have missed this the first time? Then, one thing caught his eye. Sitting in the middle of the living room was the widest, nicest, and newest television on the market. He knew that he didn't buy it, and in fact, he had no clue as to how it got into the home.

Amazed, he walked to the massive screen and found a note that read *A gift for you*. Next to that was a stack of videos that read *Purposeful Identity*. Barely able to think, he pressed the power button. Then his excitement faded. The TV didn't work. "Why?" he asked. "Why doesn't it work?"

"Plug it in," the father's voice said from behind him.

He turned and ran to his father and hugged him. Tears poured down his cheeks. The father smiled, crying himself, and said, "I know all you've done, but I forgive you, my son. If you trust me, I can show you what you were looking for. First, you must know that you're my child. Second, I have something I wish to show you: your true identity. Go and plug in the cord."

Then someone knocked on the door. The son opened it to see a massive body, brawny and intimidating, standing there looking a bit angry: the mystery man. "What are you doing here?" the son said.

Hiding his anger, the mystery man deceptively replied, "That is my television, so please go grab it for me. Okay, my boy?"

In a moment of confusion, the son thought that it could possibly be true. It made sense, since he hadn't purchased the TV, and so he went to grab it. But the father reminded him, "This home was built and given to you out of my love, and it is yours, as is the TV and everything else in it. Turn it on and tell this man to leave. He is the Identity Thief. He has come here to try to stop you from finding your purpose."

The thief could hear the father too and began shouting all he could to persuade the son otherwise. "This isn't your home! You don't deserve this house! The television is mine! You can't tell me to leave! I'm more powerful than you! Give it and all you have to me, and I'll give you an even better house and purpose than your father can!"

At once the son could see that everything the Identity Thief was saying was a lie. He remembered what the Identity Thief had said before about finding what it was that he was searching for. Everything he'd uttered was a lie. For the first time in a long time, the son believed in his father and told the thief to leave. He closed the door, sat down on the couch, pressed the power button, and changed the channel so the father could show him his true identity.

The father gazed lovingly into his son's eyes, which were now filled with gratitude that streamed down his face in the form of tears. The overjoyed father placed his hand on his shoulder, and the son grasped his father's hand.

Your beliefs can kill you or give you life. The choice is yours. So what do you believe?

TOOL #10: WHAT DO YOU BELIEVE?

Take a few minutes and write down what your beliefs are and what they are rooted in. Ask yourself, is this something I would die for?

_____

_____

_____

_____

_____

_____

_____

_____

_____

_____

_____

_____

_____

_____

_____

_____

_____

SIX

Question #5.5 - Why?

"*Winners never quit, and quitters never win.*"
— VINCE LOMBARDI

"*He who has a why to live can bare almost any how.*"
— FRIEDRICH NIETZSCHE

INTRODUCTION TO WHY

Above all, words and words alone separate us from animals. I've heard you can (to some extent) raise a puppy and baby similarly. "No! Don't touch this. Don't do that. That's a no-no." Then, when the little girl is around two years old, right before their eyes, something extraordinary happens for Mom and Dad. The child they have been giving orders to looks them in the eye and says, "No!" Mom and Dad break out laughing. The look on her face, her little lips pursed and eyes sincere, is just too much for them. It was her best impression of Mom and Dad. The child has done something beautiful.

Let another year or two pass, and now she is messing up grammar, saying words she shouldn't, and even putting together sentences that are too long for her good. Then, out of nowhere, without warning, the child learns the power of asking *why*. "Why do dogs bark?" "Why does poop smell?" "Why are people so tall?" "Why is the earth so big?" "Why do you have big ears?" "Why do you have hair on your face?" "Why do you love me?"

When a child learns the power of *why*, it seems they ask that question every day. I used to ask it every day too. In my younger years, without noticing and for some unknown reason at the time, I stopped asking. There was a shift in my youthful mind from being filled with wonder, mystery, and desire to know everything, to being filled with certain doubts, a realist attitude, and believing that I had most if not all the answers.

You see, I think that *why* is one of the best discovery words in the world. When we ask a question, typically we want an answer. I have found that using *why* is so powerful. It can shut up a know-it-all in a moment, plunge a student into an hour of deep thought, or simply get you the answer you want. For instance, try asking, "Why do I exist?" "Why are humans different from dogs?" "Why am I alive?" "Why do I work here?" The power of asking why is far-reaching. Still, given this truth, many, just as I did, abandon the potential of being a *why* person and become something like a *Because* person.

Someone who adopts the mindset of a *Because* person slowly loses their capacity to learn. To make things more complicated, the *Because* person has little power to influence another positively. Here's why. I've heard a person answer a compelling question such as "Why do you exist?" with "Because I do." Can you see as clearly as I can, how detrimental answers like that can be to a purposeful identity? There is no limit on how much it can hinder a person's ability to understand their God-given strengths, weaknesses, passions, brand, and beliefs. Beware of the *Because*-person mentality. I urge you to rediscover the power of asking why. For example:

Student: "Why do moms have babies, but dads don't?"
Teacher: "Because they do."
Student: "Why are you so tall when I'm so short?"
Teacher: "Because you are."

Student: "Why do you work a job that you hate?"

Teacher: "Because I do."

Student: "Why do you say *because* so much?"

Teacher: "Because."

When *because* is the precedent for a person's answer, they either haven't thought the question through, or they don't have a clue. When a curious child asks a question such as "Why don't dogs talk when they are two years old?" a simple "Because they don't" isn't going to do. They don't talk because they weren't made in the image and likeness of God as we are. This is question #5.5 that everybody must answer to discover purposeful identity. Intentional, thoughtful, and sincere answers are required—and now I ask the question, *why?*

LESSONS TO REFLECT ON

As an adult, I rediscovered the power of why. I plan on harnessing it for the rest of my life, and truthfully, I hope you do too. But before you can begin harnessing its power, you need to adopt the mindset of a child. In Matthew 18:3, Jesus said, "Truly I tell you, unless you change and become like little children, you will never enter the kingdom of heaven."

I believe becoming like little children means to stop thinking we know it all, to stop judging one another, and to stop disposing of crucial questions we face in our lives. In addition, I believe becoming like a child again is wanting to learn. Think about a toddler as a seemingly empty vessel. In this case, the vessel holds liquid knowledge, wisdom, intelligence, faith, etc. The vessel, apart from a few splashes, is pretty much empty. As the child grows, people will undoubtedly pour into them.

Friends, parents, teachers, and others, even ourselves, will teach us everything that they believe we need to know. All our experiences and relationships are so different that no two of us receive the same fill, although we receive from the same water source. As we grow, we continue to fill up until one day we become adults and reach our maximum level. Then the filling stops.

I believe Jesus was saying to become like little children for a specific reason. The purpose of the command is to reveal how the world has filled us. There is a need to be refilled by something else. Our friends, family, and even ourselves have gone to the town's river to get the water, then directly filled our vessel. There is no cleaning of the water or purifying it. We have simply put the bacteria-saturated, virus-infested water into our vessels. Remember, question 4 about the brand—and how the young man in the movie wanted to please the world? That desire drove him to please the world because that's what filled his vessel. When we allow ourselves to be full of the world's water, our bodies become sick from all the diseases, impurities, and viruses in it.

To become like little children again means to be drained of the dirty water—the water from which we will experience thirst over and over again—and to be reborn and be filled by living water. That divine water is water from which we will never thirst again. Jesus was saying that what we have inside has to be poured out so that we can be filled with what he has to offer. So many people have their hearts locked and sealed up. Their sickly vessels are filled to the brim with the river's murky water, and the lid capped. No one can change their mind. They already know all they need to know. They are a *Because* person.

When something doesn't make sense to a child, they ask why. "Why are there so many starving children in the world?" The last thing I want to say to that child is, "Because there are." I would much rather say, "Children are starving for many reasons, yet none of them are okay. The best thing we can do is whatever we may be able to do for them." As a father of three, and a life coach, mentor, and pastor, I've found that children love to learn. Their vessels are empty and desire to be filled.

I can tell by how their eyes light up when they receive the answer that their soul so deeply sought after. Young adults who ask questions are filled with the same awe and joy upon receiving their answer. There is no secret. Ask, and you shall receive. Receive what? The knowledge, wisdom, understanding, and power that are necessary to do something with what you have been given in life. The power of *why* can break the seal off those vessels that have been locked up.

As well, before you can begin harnessing the power of *why*, you need to know it's okay to become like a kid again and start asking why. Why do you have strengths, weaknesses, passions, a brand, and beliefs? Why think about them at all? Why do they matter? Why care at all about investing in yourself? The answer I have found that trumps all others is, to find your purposeful identity.

The apostle Peter said, "Once you had no identity as a people; now you are God's people. Once you received no mercy; now you have received God's mercy" (1 Peter 2:10 NLT). It is through God's mercy and grace that he refills us. Not with physical water but with spiritual living water, which has no maximum fill level. We can continue to grow and learn all the days of our lives so long as we wish.

Learning is one of my favorite experiences. Although the lesson itself might not be so delightful, what comes from such lessons seems to always benefit my life, and asking questions such as "Why?" goes together with learning lessons. Life lessons are essential. As a parent, all I strive for is to be able to teach my children such lessons. I have learned that some lessons require time; even so, the end product is still beautiful.

Think of a caterpillar becoming a butterfly. A butterfly's average lifespan is typically only a couple of months (given factors such as changing weather patterns, predators, and diseases), and the transformation from caterpillar to butterfly can take up to a month itself, if not longer. The caterpillar can spend half of its life "slugging" around searching for food while it waits and waits and waits in hopes of one day swirling up in a cocoon. Half of its life is waiting! That is slow and drawn out, wouldn't you say?

Now, what exactly is it waiting for? Well, caterpillars have a specific hormone called juvenile hormone. When levels are high, the juvenile hormone tells the caterpillar to remain a caterpillar. When the hormone levels fall, nearly down to zero, this signals the caterpillar to find a place and prepare. It is the hormone level that dictates when each caterpillar will be ready to be transformed. Time alone is not in control of this process. To use a real-life example, think of it like saying to your teenager(s) the seemingly incomprehensible word "No!" All you want to know is why don't they listen when you say it.

Who out there honestly thought that such a simple word, *no*, would bring about confusion, rebellion, and disregard from a child? Maybe teens genuinely don't understand the meaning of *no*. Perhaps they won't for years. Quite possibly, they show no hope of coming around. Probably in many households, the teens acquiesce every time Mom or Dad shout it. More likely, they storm off, shouting back all kinds of words. Either way, each time they hear the dreadful "No!" something is turned off, and the lesson isn't transmitting. Or is it? For years and years, Mom and Dad battle their hormonal teens.

Then everything changes a decade or two down the road when their kids have children of their own. The new young parents' hormone levels are well-tamed by now. However, no one could have prepared them for what is to come: their children begin touching things, *everything* they shouldn't (like outlets, chemicals, and knives). With few options, all that new Mom and new Dad can do is hatch from the cocoon and shout, "No!"

Upon seeing their child's reaction, the young parents realize, *Wow! All those years, Mom and Dad said no for my good!* The entire experience is revolutionary, just like a caterpillar becoming a butterfly. The best moments are when we grandparents get the chance to hear our kids tell their kids, "No!" Even better is when those little ones hit that two-year-old mark and say it back. Why do lessons like this take so much time? I think of it as an artist transforming a blank canvas into a masterpiece. Every stroke matters, and above all, it is the final image that matters.

During the entire process of transformation, there is always going to be a filling occurring for Mom, Dad, and child. Now, if Mom and Dad "flip a lid" every time the child doesn't listen, the child will undoubtedly be filled with the world's water. On the contrary, if the parents seek wisdom from God during the process, the Lord will enable them to see past their present behavior and see the child for the blessing they are. This revelation will fill the parents with patience and love, which in turn can lead to a fondness of the teaching process.

We shouldn't cut corners with kids. They know when we care about teaching them versus quickly telling them something simply to get them out of our faces. This example is dear to my heart because when we stop genuinely filling our kids, they will turn to someone or something they think will, but these people too often are carrying the world's water. Even though the kids' not understanding *no* doesn't seem so important in their younger years, there are older kids who are lost, perhaps on drugs, rebellious, or even filled with hate. These experiences can be so hard for a parent to go through, and my heart goes out to you if that is your situation. The power of *why* is more than just a one-time cure-all. Sometimes it requires continual asking and building until one day everything is clear.

Romans 5:3–5 ESV reminds us, "More than that, we rejoice in our sufferings, knowing that suffering produces endurance, and endurance produces character, and character produces hope, and hope does not put us to shame, because God's love has been poured into our hearts through the Holy Spirit who has been given to us."

WHY LESSONS MATTER

Lessons are what give us the opportunity to learn, apply that learning, and, ultimately, become transformed. I hope you have learned some key lessons while reading this book. This book was written with the intention that the reader might not only learn something helpful from it, but also experience moments of genuine self-discovery. It has been a constant hope of mine that you'll close this book as a person who truly knows who they are and why they were crafted.

My favorite tool, a Snapshot of You, ties in every question we've considered. Its purpose is to help you reflect on what you've identified about yourself and your purpose. Remember this: when we know who we're crafted to be, we then are enabled to help those who are suffering and lost. Every person must come to discover *who* they are and *why* they are here.

. . .

WHY THESE 5.5 QUESTIONS?

Strength

Terry Fox was the runner with one leg who represented what strength can accomplish when plugged in. Strengths are given to us to enable us to push through challenging times. They are like hidden diamonds; often, they reside deep inside and we haven't yet discovered them, but we must find them nonetheless.

Weakness

Nick Vujicic is the evangelist with no arms or legs whose extraordinary life demonstrates that a personal weakness doesn't have to limit our life. He once felt like a child who was lost and lonely, but he later found his strength in Jesus. He proved to the world that weaknesses don't belong on our resumes and do not define us.

Passion

My lawn passion was really a passion, yet it wasn't my purposeful passion. Purposeful passion has two components: internal passion and external passion. Internal passion is what gets us up in the morning. External passion is what breaks our heart. Both have been deposited into our heart, and we must find them and act on them.

Brand

Harriet Tubman was freed from the false labels imposed on her, and created her brand. Our brands can be authentic and genuine or more like fake cheese. What we allow inside will determine what comes out. If we put fake in, fake is what comes out. If we put truth in, truth comes out. Our brands depend on our name. Our name is built upon consistency. We are consistently fighting for a cause, consistency in character, and consistency in beliefs.

Belief

Then we looked at the importance of placing our complete trust in the Master Sculptor; he has big plans for you, me, and everyone else in the world. When we're going the wrong way, we hope someone tackles us and stops us from making the wrong choice. Our beliefs affect every aspect of our life. Do you feed the hungry, degrade the worth of other people, or fight for a just cause? Either way, our beliefs are the number one factor that determines the kind of human being that we're choosing to be. And now, *why*?

Why?

Does any of this matter? It absolutely does! That is, if you want to live a purposeful and fulfilled life. Your true identity lies within the answers to each of these questions. The deeper you look, the more unique you will see you are. No two thumbprints match. No two hearts match either. Although they are all similar, each one has individual features. Within the answers to these 5.5 questions, there are similarities that we all have, but figuring out your own answers will reveal your identity and distinguish you from everybody else. Tool #11 can help you see yourself more clearly than ever before.

TOOL #11: SNAPSHOT OF YOU

The past 5.5 questions, when answered honestly and intentionally, are powerful awareness builders. If you've gone through the book and written down the answers to each question, then you've already begun equipping yourself. Take your answers and write a descriptive paragraph about what you have discovered about yourself. These questions will provide you with a snapshot of who you are today, at least in your own eyes.

1. What are your strengths?
2. What are your weaknesses?
3. What are you passionate about?
4. What is your brand?
5. What do you believe?

Here is what my Snapshot looked like when I originally did it:

My name is Joe Pellegrino. My strengths include public speaking, teaching, coaching, leadership, perseverance, creativity, drive, and vision. My weaknesses are self-confidence, writing, and detailed work. I sometimes struggle with integrity and saying no to others. I am passionate about seeing others, especially men, become all they were created to be. I am also passionate about my family, whom I love very much. I also love the game of baseball, through which I have learned so much about life. At one time, my brand was not good, but I now believe that has all changed. People who know me believe I am a man who cares very much about others and wants to see them attain purpose and success in their lives, and that I will do what I can to help them get there. I also believe people trust me and that if I say I will do something, it will be done. I believe in the words of the Bible and therefore believe that Jesus is the Savior of the world. I believe I was made for a purpose, and that is why I do what I do. I believe this because I have gone through life with me being the focus, and nothing ever worked. While I experienced success, there was never true fulfillment or joy. After studying the Scriptures and opening my eyes to the world around me, I saw the truth. My belief system allowed me to unleash a purposeful identity in my life.

Now compose your Snapshot of You (use another sheet of paper if necessary):

_____

_____

_____

_____

_____

WHY CONCLUSION: WHAT'S YOUR WHY ANSWER?

What's your *why* answer? I mean, have you thought about it? A lot of people haven't even considered, let alone thoughtfully examined, this incredibly significant question. Let me tell you, it deserves to be examined! If you're feeling somewhat lost, you need to ask, "Why?" and become as a little child again and find your authentic personhood. Then you will see great things happen in your life.

How come some people rise and achieve great success in fields where there are dozens if not hundreds of "competitors"? Why did Martin Luther King Jr. become the preeminent leader of the civil rights movement? He was not the only African-American man speaking out on the matter; many others were as well. He was not the only preacher in the world either. So what about this man did people identify with and cling to? What was he willing to live and die for without raising a fist? It was his *why*.

If you've listened to the "I Have a Dream" speech, you'll hear this great leader's heart—his *why*. You see, he learned the hard way that the civil rights movement was more significant than he was. It would take time and dedication to see change. And how would he go about accomplishing this change? He first had to know his purpose. His purpose was to serve the cause to the point that he knew it could cost him his life. Martin Luther King Jr. knew what was demanded of him, and without knowing the power of *why*, there's no other reason he could've been courageous enough to fulfill his purpose.

Dr. King was confronted by the deeply rooted and foundationally significant problem of racial bigotry in our country. He had to make a decision. Yet the decision could only be made if he first asked, "Why? Why am I going to do this? Why am I going to risk my life for those suffering all around me?"

Once he received his answer, he made the decision to live for his purpose. Now, why did others cling to his vision? The people saw he was filled with truth, genuineness, and conviction. They not only knew his answers as to why he was doing this, but his *why* became their *why*. Why should blacks have the same rights as whites? The answer would seem so obvious from our more recent perspective, but historically, it was a radical and unpopular concept. The quest for freedom tragically cost many people their lives.

Why did this one man rise up to take the lead and change so many lives in the process, while countless others stayed silent? In his "I Have a Dream" speech, you can see why. It was not because it was a great speech (although great it was). Motivational speakers give great speeches, and within a couple of weeks, the same people who left fired-up for life are often in dire need of a revival. The real reason Dr. King's speech was so successful is that he boldly declared his *why*. If you listen to the speech, he didn't just paint a moving picture of blacks and whites living peacefully together, although he does say that living in mutual respect and unity is the goal. He does more. The visionary leader always led his audience to *why*. Don't let this elude you. For example, each time, he pointed out that there was "withering injustice." He wasn't just saying life for blacks in this country wasn't fair. No. He was showing people everywhere why it's important to no longer accept withering injustice as the status quo.

People were suffering, and cultural bigots, if not bad enough, were becoming extreme racists. Despite that daunting reality, Dr. King's *why* was even more powerful than all the opposition could muster. Blacks weren't only being mistreated individually; for decades, all of the rules were constructed such that they couldn't hope to rise higher in American society as a whole. Systemic injustice!

Dr. King was both a visionary leader and a teacher. With great eloquence, he let the nation and the world know that the concept of justice in and of itself demands equality. Anything less would be like fake cheese (to use our earlier example). It would be a check marked "insufficient funds." Anything less than complete equality would be "withering injustice"—a cruel mockery of the very principles that the Founding Fathers sacrificed and died for.

His *why* was so clearly portrayed in his speech, and so powerful, that the "I Have a Dream" speech is often credited as the pivotal point in civil rights history. That's powerful! And it all rested on his *why*. I can picture him, standing in front of the mirror only days before the monumental speech, looking deeply into his own eyes with keen intensity and asking himself, "Why are you doing this? You and your family will surely face great danger. Why, Martin? Why?"

Such injustices broke his heart; they were his *external passion*. The hope for seeing a better world was his *internal passion*; it got him up each morning and kept him going even when times were tough. He knew he would use speech, one of his strengths, to battle such injustice. He knew he would have to overcome his weakness of vulnerability in the context of Southern society (lack of adequate police protection and prosecution against hate crimes was something that blacks endured daily) for there to be success.

In 1956 his house was bombed. Just a couple of years later, he was stabbed by a woman and almost died. And in 1963 he was attacked on stage by a white supremacist. None of these attacks mattered. He decided where he stood, he was not a *because of* person but a *why* person. He knew the cost of his calling but never quit through all the trials of vulnerability. In fact they became the source of his courage. He was resilient, bold, tenacious, and yet peaceful. These became pillars of his brand.

Then, the "I Have a Dream" speech revealed what he believed. He believed his four children would be able to live in a nation where they were not judged by the color of their skin but rather the content of their character. He believed that white and black children would be able to join hands in school. He believed one day every valley would be exalted, that every mountain and all the rough places would be made plain, that the crooked places would be made straight, and that the glory of the Lord would be revealed and that *all* flesh would be able to see it together. In his own words, this faith would bring about a "stone of hope." Wow! His very life became the reason we need to answer these questions. He was able to reveal his *why* through his strengths, weaknesses, passions, brand, and beliefs.

Martin Luther King Jr. gave his life for a cause that was focused on teaching a life lesson. A lesson the teacher so badly yearned wouldn't have to be experienced by the next generation. Over the decades, positive changes have happened in this country and rightfully so. It is evident that Dr. King's dream has not yet been fully realized, but his sacrifices and visionary leadership laid the essential foundation for changes yet to come. How wonderful it is that there are still many students, even today, wanting to learn Martin Luther King Jr.'s lesson. The changes that have taken place to date were only able to happen because Dr. King was deeply moved by the reality that his community and his country were in dire trouble.

He would either respond or be silent. Some whisperers said that giving his speech could be life-threatening, but that possibility didn't stop him. The whispers turned out to be correct, but he wouldn't accept the fear-driven alternative to sit quietly by while injustice ensued. Martin Luther King Jr. was a man who knew his purposeful identity and decided to answer his call. His internal and external passions worked together in his heart, and as a result, he issued a nationwide call to action that reverberated internationally to right a significant moral wrong.

Well, friends, we now find ourselves in a moment like the past where our country is in turmoil. We are facing a massive identity crisis. Who will step up?

Answering these crucial questions, learning their lessons, and discovering your purposeful identity is the only way this crisis can be stopped. The very reason I wrote this book is that as we answer these all-important questions, we can see the most critical question hovering with the rest: why? It is only when we know why and that *why* is lived can someone find their purposeful identity.

SEVEN

Identity

"*Be yourself; everyone else is* already *taken.*"
— OSCAR WILDE

IDENTITY MANIA IN AMERICA

To quote Damian Marley, son of the famous musician Bob Marley, "Everybody wants to be somebody."[1] Welcome to the next century. Everybody wants to be somebody, and many unconsciously wish to be told who that "somebody" is, rather than ask the questions and find out the truth of who they are.

If you're aware and open to this reality, the evidence of people fighting to identify with one thing or another will begin to flood your thoughts. It's astonishing how strong this inner desire for identity is. People are willing to identify with anything, so long as it makes sense to them. For instance, are you a Coke or a Pepsi person? Football or baseball enthusiast? Boy or girl? Oreo or Chips Ahoy person? Ford or Chevy? Left-wing or right-wing? American or Russian? Mountain climber or couch potato? Mr. High Energy or Miss Social Butterfly?

Marketing and branding experts have recognized, exploited, and channeled this inner desire for identity for a great number of years.

This legitimate need has not escaped the notice of sociologists, politicians, and even religious cults. The manipulation and exploitation of this deep longing has caused a dangerous tidal wave of identity confusion in America.

There's an urgency for discovering and living out authentic identity in America. The success of both the current and the next generation depends on it. Marriages are failing at an alarming rate, young people are dropping out of school, drugs are more prevalent, mental disorders are reaching historic highs, and so much more. People are lost. So long as people adopt a humanistic, me-centered identity, things will only get worse. People who don't know who they are often do drastic things. Think about mid-life crises and how many bad decisions are often made in that season. Sooner or later, the hollowness of adopting who others say you are will become evident. Such people frequently don't know what to do or who they really are, and as a result, they simply collapse, often abandoning their family or becoming emotionally disconnected. I've seen it happen.

It's time to reverse this loss of self and start making identity gains. Most people in America are fighting this confusion battle right now. The good news is anyone who lets in the truth will be set free! Today can be your day. Our true identity resides within our core self, our unique DNA. Our very design demands the recognition of this simple yet profound fact. The marketers and politicians have capitalized on an already-present need for identity; they didn't create the need. The yearning for identity is within us and active from the day we are born. The closer a person grows to God and the more fulfilled they become, the closer they are to finding their true identity.

Maybe you're in that fight right now. Perhaps it's a massive problem for you. Don't give up. Answering these 5.5 questions will start you on your journey to find your true self.

Within the story, the active Identity Thief is on the prowl, seeking to rob you of your potential and identity. Make no mistake, God created you for a purpose and with purpose. There is something that must come into view: your true identity.

Back in January 2019, I fulfilled one of my dreams by visiting the

Holy Land. For several days I was blessed to see the Bible come to life, and to walk in the footsteps of Jesus. We visited most of the key biblical sites. It was awesome, something I will never forget. However, one stop in Jerusalem really impacted me: the Holocaust Museum. This museum brought the story of Schindler's List to life for me. Millions of hard-working Jewish people and their families were slaughtered because of one maniac and his followers.

Now of course I knew the story, but once there, I realized what Hitler did. The people came to the concentration camps with a name and immediately were given a number, forever tattooed on their arm. He stole their identity. This was the beginning of the end for most who entered these camps. When someone is robbed of their identity, their *true* identity, it creates chaos within.

Since the beginning of time, the Identity Thief has sought to steal the identity of God's people, making them question who they are. David, son of Jesse, a small and seemingly feeble kid, was fully equipped with his identity and answered the call of God on his life. He stood up to the giant Goliath, who was slandering the Israelites. He knew his identity was found in God, and it looked like this:

> Moreover, David said, "The Lord, who delivered me from the paw of the lion and the paw of the bear, He will deliver me from the hand of this Philistine." ... Then David said to the Philistine, "You come to me with a sword, with a spear, and with a javelin. But I come to you in the name of the Lord of hosts, the God of the armies of Israel, whom you have defied. This day the Lord will deliver you into my hand, and I will strike you and take your head from you. And this day I will give the carcasses of the camp of the Philistines to the birds of the air and the wild beasts of the earth, that all the earth may know that there is a God in Israel. Then all this assembly shall know that the Lord does not save with sword and spear; for the battle is the Lord's, and He will give you into our hands."
> (1 Samuel 17:37, 45–48 NKJV)

David trusted in the Lord. The Identity Thief may be a leering giant like Goliath, but the Lord loves us and uses average Joes, just like David, to fight his battles. It doesn't matter if you're an average Joe; God wants to use you. The foundation of this book is to aid you in the discovery of both your identity *and* your purpose. Not one or the other.

We will get to purpose a bit later in our journey, but first, we must deal with some important life issues.

OUR FRIEND FAILURE

 "Only those who dare to fail greatly can ever achieve greatly."
— Robert F. Kennedy

UNDERSTANDING FAILURE

Back in the introduction, I told you about two great hardships that brought me face-to-face with who I truly was. Before I jump into these stories, I would like to:

- make a distinction between a noble failure and an unjustifiable failure,
- expose failure as being inevitable, and
- go over the failure acronym, FEAR.

NOBLE FAILURE VS. UNJUSTIFIABLE FAILURE

A close friend of mine, Dr. Dean Radtke, founder and president of the Ministry Institute, is a huge supporter of noble failure. Dr. Radtke says that noble failure sometimes is the outcome from taking big risks or stepping outside of one's comfort zone in favor of the overall goal or vision for a person or entity. He supports when failure ensues as a result of such action because he believes failing for the right cause (i.e., noble failure) is part of the process toward success.

A good example of noble failure would be the Wright brothers. These brothers had a vision to create the world's first "heavier than air" flying motor vehicle, also known as an airplane. Before attempting flight, they first hit the books and laboratory and did their research. With minimal funding, over a period of five years (1900–1905), the brothers tested various wing molds/foils, kites, and gliders to see if their wing designs were legitimate.

The brothers, often using a wind tunnel, saw firsthand what most would call failure after failure, as many of their wing designs would fail. According to NASA, over two hundred wing designs were created and tested. Before they tried their first real-time man trial, the Wright brothers had already become accustomed to failure.

This is a perfect example of noble failure. The brothers consistently encouraged each other to endure the challenging passion they shared and proceed with the testing. The result of such endurance? Well, you know.

An unjustifiable failure is far less attractive. For instance, a worker who is entrusted with making sure the nuts, bolts, and fasteners are locked and tightened on an aircraft that fails to do their job. In 1991 this very thing happened, resulting in tragedy. The National Transportation Safety Board found forty-seven missing fasteners caused a Continental Express Embraer 120 to break apart and crash.

What was distracting the worker that day? Finances, marriage stress, sickness, fatigue, ignorance? Failure usually is missing the mark. Noble failure can be justified, but missing forty-seven fasteners is an unjustifiable failure, and that day it cost many people their lives.

In life, failure is inevitable. Identifying the difference between noble failure and unjustifiable failure will ultimately build up our standard on what failure is acceptable and what is not. Knowing *why* the two are different speaks directly to our attitude and character.

FAILURE IS INEVITABLE

Is it fair to try to count how many times we have and will fail in life? Maybe not, but I'm glad that people like Thomas Edison and the

Wright brothers kept a count of the failures they experienced. It reminds me that failure isn't a one-time end-all event. More than that, their attitude in the process of failing can help us learn how to fail properly, or, as John C. Maxwell says, "failing forward."

Yes, I believe there is a right way to fail. There has to be, because everybody who attempts to achieve something in life experiences failure. People can and do ignore this fact, and as a result they end up letting life "happen" to them, rather than living the life that they could be living. I fully believe that failure has a bad reputation. Personally, I believe it is one of the key components to building a successful *anything*. When people like Edison or the Wright brothers fail, their failure is known by everyone because they are the people who I call *path pavers*, the ones who try big things that have yet to be achieved. This puts them under the microscope. By default, when trying something new, the critics' true nature comes out, and the Edisons of the world are quickly ridiculed.

What do you do if you have tried something five hundred times, like Edison, or have built two hundred prototypes and have had nothing but failure? Well, critics are path pavers too, except they're laying a path that leads to where they are: a place where life is an uneventful, and often too comfortable, totally predictable, and completely unfulfilling experience. I say listen to who God says you are and learn from the best. In order to overcome self-doubt, critical microscopes, and whispers from the Identity Thief, we must know our identity.

If the Identity Thief is the overall enemy of identity, the weapon he uses against identity is confusion, as you just read in the previous chapter, and the weapon he uses against pursuing purpose passionately is the fear of failure. With regard to failure's inevitability and how to overcome it, there are three parts to address:

- Fear of failure
- Cultural mirage crisis
- Attitude in vision

Fear of Failure

Let's be honest, the possibility of failure lurks around every corner. For many, a consistent lingering whisper of doubt follows them. We've all heard it one time or another: *No matter what you put into something, the ultimate end is failure.*

Have you ever heard fear described as the acronym FEAR: False Evidence Appearing Real? I would say believing the idea that failure is always the end result of pursuing a dream, is a good example of false evidence appearing real. I see it like this: The second a person finds their identity, they find themselves at a crossroads. Before them lies two paths, one to the left and one to the right. The road to the left represents choosing to live a life that is "safe"—predictable, easy, and probably devoid of failure. This road, due to popular demand, must be a much broader road than the other road, and it is jam packed full of people.

To the right is a road that represents "the road less traveled." It is the epitome of choosing to live a life that pursues your passions, dreams, goals, and visions in an attempt to fulfill your purposeful identity. Compared to the other overflowing road, few people are usually found on this trail. Deep in your bones, as you stare at the two paths, you know which one you want to choose. But every time you look down the road to the right, you hear a whisper that sounds something like this:

> "That life appears to be fulfilling, but you? Really? You think you have what it takes to pursue your purpose? Come on, starting a business requires money, something you don't have much of. It requires training, and you know how tough training is. And in an economy like this, you know as well as I do what's going to happen. You won't find customers, you'll get tired of trying, you'll eventually give up, and then you'll go broke. You can't take this road. Don't you see how dripping with the certainty of failure it is?"

Does this voice sound familiar?

The Identity Thief is no novice in deception. He only whispers this when you're looking down the right road, thinking about pursuing your purpose. So long as a person listens to him, they will see that one road as a sure-fire way to fail in life, while the left road will be easy living, comfortable, and seemingly failure-free.

The faulty, fear-inspired perception that the right road is bound to be saturated in failure while the easy left road is guaranteed failure-free needs to be addressed.

Cultural Mirage Crisis

Sadly, in America, simultaneously with the identity mania crisis, a cultural mirage crisis is also going on. Let me explain.

As Americans, we often have a false sense of security when it comes to living comfortably. More specifically I am referring to our jobs, food supply, water supply, freedoms, and more. Americans are beyond blessed to live in the country we do. However, when we take for granted the amenities and resources made so easily available, without thought or appreciation, we find ourselves within the *American mirage*. The resource gathering, refining, packaging, and distribution systems that had to be in place to get, say, Fritos or hairspray to the typical store counter could not be numbered. Thousands upon thousands of these systems are interconnected like a web, all across the globe.

Yet, as the leading consumer-driven culture in the world, we consume products and become consumed by the culture. Being consumed by the culture results in a deep desensitizing of our heart to the injustices in the world. The American mirage in one sense is also connected to the perception that everyone in the world has it as easy as we do—that they have a Walmart full of food, a dozen car dealers on a busy street, tens of restaurants in just a few blocks, Broadway, hospitals, pharmacies, etc. Truth is, we have it the best, which most people know. So good in fact that "poverty" in America is often identified as "upper-middle class" in many other societies.

The American mirage isn't a universal perception that we Americans have; instead, it's the byproduct that affects many people. Listening to the false whispers about what's important in life will ultimately lead any culture to be living a mirage.

I bring this reality up for one reason: sometimes things aren't as they're made out to be. Sure, by now you would readily agree that the Identity Thief is deceptive, a liar, and a manipulator when it comes to a person recognizing their identity and purpose. But do you think he's going to stop trying to pull you away from your destiny? He won't! It is his mission! He uses the American mirage for a large-scale attack on the people. His goal is to get people comfortable and complacent.

He uses another mirage for personal attacks. That is the *crossroads mirage*. Being aware of what is reality vs. what is just a mirage must be addressed. The reality for the crossroad is that no matter what road you take, both are undoubtably rooted with potential for failure. The mirage is that the left broad-and-easy road is more safe and secure than the other.

Think of a woman whose crossroad is to take the left road (a factory job molding plastic) or the right road (starting her very own hair salon). Her passion is doing hair and she's known it since she was a little girl doing her dolls' hair. As a teenager she would gladly do hair for her cousins, her mom, and many of her neighbors. Now, she's at a point where the corner store at a busy intersection just opened for rent. For years she's dreamed about that exact location being the place where she would open her first hair salon. Her crossroads became real as she stood just outside the doors, with her entire life savings in one hand and a pen to sign the lease in the other. Every muscle fiber in her body wanted to rip the door off its hinges and run inside and pursue this dream, but a familiar voice whispers:

"The life appears to be fulfilling ... but you? Really? You think you have what it takes to pursue your purpose? Come on, starting a business requires money, something you don't have enough of. It requires training, and you know how tough training is. And in an economy like this, you know as well as I do what's going to happen. You won't find customers, you'll get tired of trying, you'll eventually give up, and then you'll go broke. You can't take this road. Don't you see how dripping with the certainty of failure it is? If I were you, I would take the factory job. At least there you'll get a steady paycheck, guaranteed hours, and benefits. Do you really want to give all that up to pursue what—childhood dreams?"

The Identity Thief tries to fill her with the belief that the factory job is safe and secure. (Ask anyone post-Coronavirus if that's true.) He would say anything to keep her from pursuing her purpose with passion. He makes the factory road seem like the most comfortable road to take. But is it true?

This young woman has sat down with many advisors to discuss what it would take to operate on her own. A few things the experts agreed on were a business plan, a loan, sweat and labor, licenses and permits, and a lot of trust, to name a few essential aspects of the vision. But *trust*?

Her conversation with an advisor, which she remembers clearly, went like this:

"So, say I did my business plan, got my loan, and knew all the licenses and permits needed to operate. There must be other things to worry about?"

The advisor replied, "Sure. If you want to worry, you'll always find something to worry over. Heck, if you really wanted to, you could choose to worry about this pen. You could use it every day, get used to the feel of it, love its ink lines and more, but suddenly with one worry take all the beauty of the pen away by saying to yourself, 'What if the pen runs out of ink as I try to sign the lease?' Listen, if you're going to do this, you're going to need to trust."

"*Trust*? Trust whom?" she asked.

"God, of course."

She left that meeting feeling that she wasn't alone in this endeavor. After a long prayer, she went to the bank, withdrew all her savings, and then headed to the store.

It was outside the store, moments before she chose to pursue her dream, that the Identity Thief began whispering. He had already tried to convince her that pursuing the salon was too risky to make sense and full of too many chances to fail.

Her hand reached for the door handle.

His whispers grew shaky: "At the factory you would be an employee. All big decisions would rest on another person's shoulders. You don't want to have to make big decisions, do you?"

All she could think to say was, "I don't worry about big decisions. I trust through them." And nearly ripping the door off its hinges in her excitement, she hurried inside.

There it was, the Identity Thief trying to lure another soul down the left road. I know this is a fictional example, but spiritually this is the battle that rages when it comes to making the right decision. Accompanying the comforting realities about reliable pay, benefits, and hours, he tried to impart a false sense of security in taking the factory job.

What if the company got sold to a firm from another country and as a result, her job would be lost? How about if she sprained an ankle outside of job hours and was left without pay? Or if someone who could be paid a cheaper wage was hired and she suddenly got fired? All of these scenarios happen every day across America.

These too are potential realities that often go unrecognized, just as the work that went into getting the bottle of hairspray from the factory to the store's counter. A person can choose to be oblivious to the realities associated with the left road—the realities that lay just below surface level. Sadly, a false sense of comfort lures so many down the broad-and-easy road. How painful it would have been for this woman if she chose to work at the factory just to find out she was molding hairspray caps. Her only option to avoid the awful daily reminder would be to numb the sting. This is the reality for many who travel on the broad road.

Why don't more people take the narrow road? The reasons are too many to list, but one for certain is the ever-present fear of failure. After all, God requires faith. He doesn't hide potential failures from our vision and dreams, but what he asks is for us to trust him in working through such trials. The difference isn't that one road has failure and the other is guaranteed to be failure-free, but rather that one road requires trust and faith while the other can be traveled aimlessly and without purpose or direction.

Attitude in Vision

The right vision paired with the right attitude is essential to overcome failure. Vision to fly is what helped the Wright brothers overcome handfuls of failed attempts. But it was their vision paired with the right attitude that helped them maintain their confidence. The Identity Thief tried to tear away the confidence of the woman who dreamed of getting the hair salon, just as I'm sure he did with the Wright brothers. The fictional woman and the Wright brothers chose to lean into trust rather than doubt, and this is how each were able to make the decision at their own crossroad.

A vision foreshadowed with so much potential for failure and such a slim chance for success becomes more of a nightmare than a dream for many people. What do we all do with our nightmares? Flee! (Except for you gladiators out there who slice your nightmares in two.)

The truth is so many people who have found their identity choose not to pursue their purpose because of the fear of failure. So many times this is just a mirage. Many people who never chose to pursue their purpose could have gone on to be great leaders, innovators, or creators of beautiful things. Instead of taking a chance on living a fulfilled life, they allow themselves to grow numb to what they are passionate about. For so many, the decision to practically give up on living life, to blend in with the crowds, avoid trials at any cost, and move with the spirit of the culture, is far more comfortable than taking the challenging road.

Do you think it was easy to create two hundred types of wing designs? Probably not. But even more than just designing, which minimally requires a pencil and paper, the Wright brothers had to then get each piece carved and delicately put the wing designs together. Then each wing design had to be tested separately, their outcomes recorded, and the process repeated. Was this easy? Certainly not. But building such models was the brothers' passion. When you move in the direction of your passion, your entire attitude on failure changes. Failure at this point becomes a part of the learning process. With each failure, the Wright brothers learned something new and applied it to the next test. The entire refining process (just as Edison said the lightbulb was a one-thousand-step process) is what led to the eventual success.

It's like a vehicle in its operation. If you put the right fuel in the tank, the entire system functions more efficiently. If a person has the right attitude, is fueled by hope, has a clear vision, and trusts in the Lord, there is nothing the Identity Thief can whisper to pull them away from their destiny.

TOOL #12: FAILURE FOR THOUGHT

In just a few pages, you'll read about two of my biggest failures/trials in life. I believe it's so important to remember times such as these for the sole purpose of edifying oneself. How did it feel to make it through the trial? And if you didn't make it through, what did you learn from it? Failure has a bad reputation, yet it's one of the few things in life that no matter what happens, a positive thing can be learned, regardless of the outcome.

Take a moment and write down your top two failures in life (use some details, no one but you has to read this) and see the lessons they have imparted to you, no matter their nature, from your perspective (positive or negative).

Failure 1: _____

_____

_____

What was the outcome? _____

What did you learn? _____

How have you used this to make you a better person? _____

_____

If not, how could you? _____

Failure 2: _____

_____

_____

_____

_____

What was the outcome? _____

What did you learn? _____

How have you used this to make you a better person? _____

If not, how could you? _____

_____

_____

_____

TOOL #13: TWO-PATHS VENN DIAGRAM

Failure in some way or other is inevitable. I urge you not to allow the false reality of pursuing a comfortable life, to put at risk the hope of living a fulfilled life.

Below is a Venn diagram partially filled out with what I believe are unique to each road, and also those that are congruent between each road. If you're at a crossroads as to which direction to go, take an honest look at what each path offers. Put your dream—for example, producing a movie—on the right side. Now put the other option—such as accepting a promotion at CVS—on the left. Then fill in the rest.

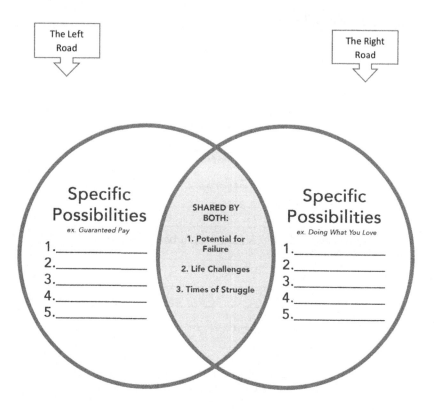

Which road do you want to choose? Circle: *Left* or *Right*

FAILURE AND ATTITUDE

Now that I have proposed, hopefully convincingly, that failure is inevitable no matter what direction a person chooses in life, I would now like to walk you to a characteristic of failure that most *fail* to recognize: it's all about attitude!

Attitude is the one piece of ourselves that we have full control of. Winston Churchill once said, "Success is stumbling from failure to failure without losing enthusiasm."[2] And I couldn't agree with him more. Success is not never having failed, but it is learning how to fail the right way and use the failure as a building block, all while maintaining the right attitude.

Maintaining the right attitude during trials has always helped me get through tough times. Pretending a trial is far off is not reality. Yet when it strikes, I firmly believe there's a way to use its very own momentum to your advantage. I've found that there's a way to position yourself to flip failure into a kind of success, kind of like a skilled UFC fighter who uses his opponent's own attack to create a counter. In my life I've faced two monstrous moments of failure. In the case of each, I had to work through to overcome the failure.

OVERCOMING FAILURE

There's no doubt that we've all failed. The truth is, many of us don't know how to work through failure, especially big failures. My hope is that sharing a couple of my valley experiences will give you the assurance that if you have ever faced, are facing, or may face times such as these, you can get through them.

A Mountain of Debt

I've always had a fire in me to do big things. From dreams of playing Major League Baseball, to visions of being an independent boss running a company, I have always been a visionary. My break came in 1986. A headhunter had gotten me an interview with a company I would have liked to work with. After our phone call, things felt right. After the interview, things felt great until the headhunter called back and told me I had been passed up for a better-qualified person.

This was tough for me because the interview felt smooth, and the company showed interest in me. Failure is always hard to swallow, so when she said, "But the company has another position open and would like to interview you for it," I was all too ready to scream, "Yes, please!" My hope was restored. Hey, perhaps the person they hired over me was truly the real deal, and this was their way of showing me that I was worth their time.

Those were my thoughts until the headhunter called me back after the second interview assuring me of the same result. I was passed up again. Surprisingly, they offered me another interview for yet another position. I figured they liked me. Determined not to fail a third time, I took it. Horrifically, the same result occurred. Three times I had been passed up for a more-qualified individual. So, when she asked if I would be interested in interviewing for another position, I couldn't say no. Well, guess what? It happened again. This time it all hit me, and I won't lie, I cried. Four times I was passed up. I felt so defeated. Regardless of the fact that they thought well enough of me to find a fit, I felt like an utter failure.

Soon after this, my current job gave me a promotion. It was nice and I was very appreciative of it, but I still felt like that wasn't my place. My heart was looking for an opportunity. Then the phone rang. There was something unusual in the works that I couldn't grasp. The lady had called looking for my old boss, whose position I ended up being promoted to. She was a headhunter, and when I told her he was no longer with the company, she asked if I would be interested in moving, began to tell me about a position, and asked if I would be interested in going for an interview. I said yes.

I ended up getting the job after a sit-down interview with a man named Arnie, the vice president of the company. For the next couple of years, Arnie took me under his wing. Every six months Arnie would get a new opportunity and would take me along. We went from company to company, much like consultants. With each move came a significant jump in salary. In the end, it was as if I had been put through a rapid business mentoring program. I felt ready to go on my own and did. In 1989 I began working for myself and have ever since.

I had been mentored by a man who showed me the ropes, and by moving from small business to small business I was exposed to all facets of how to run a company. I had always had the fire to do it and now felt ready.

Turns out I wasn't ready. I struggled for four years and then found success with my new company, Surtech Marketing. I, along with a partner, created one of the first polling systems using touchtone phones. I would sell the system to newspapers. On one sales call I met a man who knew my wife and we became fast friends. He helped me build my business and asked if I would consider joining his newspaper. I agreed and helped rebuild that newspaper. We ended up selling it to a dotcom business on a stock deal for roughly $2 million.

I also sold Surtech Marketing in a cash sale, which led me to start my dream company in 1998. It was a multimedia company designed to do something no one else had done to that point: bring together four types of media into one seamless marketing package. It was the height of the tech stock boom, so when I announced we were going to sell stock, we quickly raised around $1.3 million. It was effortless!

Things started out good. But in April 2000, it turned bad. Very bad. We were failing. *Bankruptcy* was a word floating around the table. The board of directors decided to file for corporate bankruptcy. I remember telling my wife I didn't want to file for bankruptcy because I didn't think it was biblical. But I owned only 31 percent of the company, and the board voted otherwise. I couldn't believe it. I lost not just a business, but my job, my livelihood, and financial support for my family.

Now, there was roughly $200,000 of corporate debt that was going to flow into that bankruptcy. As if I was led to do it, for some crazy reason, I expressed to my wife that I wanted to take on and pay back the business's debt. After all, I knew some of the people who put their hard-earned money into the company and trusted me. I couldn't let them down. Without blinking an eye, my wife did what any great wife would do: she supported me and agreed we should take it on personally.

To say the least, taking on a couple hundred thousand dollars of debt without a job, after losing every penny to my name, with a mortgage and three little mouths to feed, was paralyzing. But I knew it the right thing to do. Faithful? Yeah, that word works too. I was faithful to what I believed.

During this time, my integrity and character were both tested. As it turns out, taking on that debt was the best decision of my life. No doubt it was tough. Many nights I lost sleep, and many days were filled with worry. But overcoming everything, I put my faith in Jesus. Slowly but surely, he brought my family and me out of that valley of failure, and I became a better man from it. Without going through that trial, I wouldn't have been able to encourage men and women the way I have been able to.

Sometimes as people, we have dreams, big dreams to do big things. I'm that kind of person. The idea of doing something great, at least in my mind, always stimulates excitement and anticipation about the possibility of moving from something good to something great—much like the class valedictorian who aspires to become the president of the United States of America.

Taking on the mountain of debt showed me that in life, sometimes we need to move from broken to good and then from good to great. It's like a fatherless, uneducated, and mediocre athlete miraculously making it into college, then on to the big leagues. Great things often require time and trust.

When I accepted the obligation to pay back the debt myself, I was immediately plunged into the valley of failure. I couldn't be oblivious to $200,000 worth of debt, even if I tried. As challenging as I knew it would be, inside of me lay the conviction that I had chosen the right road, regardless of the mountain of debt ahead of me.

It wasn't until I conquered that mountain (with a bit of help along the way from a few true friends) that I realized I'd just stepped onto level ground. New peaks were revealed. There are steps we need to take in life to get to where we are meant to be. Rather than fleeing in the direction of the easy road, I urge you to dream first of climbing over the mountain, which lays down the right road. And if it's a mountain of debt, don't worry. I'm living proof that you can do it!

A Glove without a Hand Is Just a Glove

If you know me, you know I love baseball. The *crack* of the bat, the *thump* of a ball striking a glove—start to finish I love it. Unless the Yankees lose. That, not so much. However, even if you know nothing about baseball, still there's something to be learned from a player and his glove.

A baseball glove is an addition to the hand. And the glove-making process is no simple feat. First, the leather is specifically chosen and studied for blemishes or scars. Then it is cut, stamped, and embroidered. That seems basic, but it's not all. The leather is brought to the stitching table, where every hand-cut piece is stitched together in just the right spot. It's heated to two hundred fifty degrees and placed on a mold and hit with a mallet for the glove to obtain the right shape and align appropriately. Then the outside shell and inside liner are married, and the glove is beaten again to soften the leather. Finally, it is rubbed with oil and shipped out.

Every knot, every crease, and every piece of leather is intricately brought together. The glove is so essential. My father had a glove from the 1950s. It shows its age, and by looking at it, you wonder how he caught anything with it. How has it lasted this long?

In 2011 my home flooded. This was the second major mountain I would have to face in my life. First I lost my business; this time I lost the use of my house. Just about everything on the first floor and in the basement was destroyed or severely damaged. Furniture, pictures, memories, you name it.

Ironically, I found my dad's glove, which had been underwater for a few days. After things settled and we went through the carnage, we ended up throwing most things away. And even though this glove was badly damaged and smelled of sewer water, I couldn't part with it because it reminds me of my dad and a simpler time. It also reminds me of a time when I felt tattered, battered, bruised, and beaten. No, I couldn't throw the glove away; it was a metaphor for my life. It didn't matter what valley this flood washed me and my family into, we were going to climb out of it.

You see, a glove without a hand is just a glove, but with the right hand, it has a purpose. Even though it may not understand why it has been beaten with a mallet, put under two-hundred-fifty-degree heat, beaten up once again, and then thrown under the bed, there's a specific purpose behind all of that. It was to prepare the glove, to make it ready for use—and what hand is better than the best in the industry, the Master's hand, the hand of God.

EIGHT

Purpose

WHAT'S MY PURPOSE?

To God, you're like the best glove on the market. You're made of the most beautiful leather and stitching. If that much work goes into making a baseball glove, how much more has gone into you? Ephesians 2:10 tells us, "For we are God's handiwork, created in Christ Jesus to do good works, which God prepared in advance for us to do."

Each one of us has been created to do good works that God himself prepared in advance for us to do! This speaks to our purpose. As a Christian, I believe that the Bible, the Word of God, speaks to two types of purpose: general purpose and specific purpose.

GENERAL PURPOSE

Within this category of general purpose, I believe there are two subcategories. The first is to love your God and your neighbor. The second is to tell others the good news of Jesus Christ.

1. "He answered: 'Love the Lord your God with all your heart and with all your soul and with all your strength and with all your mind'; and, 'Love your neighbor as yourself'" (Luke 10:27).

2. Now, you may be asking, "Practically, how do I do this?" The best thing any of us can do is read the Bible and pray. Loving God and your neighbor means caring for your sick elderly mother or baking a tray of cookies for your neighbors' daughter on her birthday. It's being the best parent, friend, or mentor you can be. It's all about the heart. We show our consideration for others by what we say but more so by what we do. It is filling the heart with love and then spilling that love out—first to God in genuine devotion, and then to our neighbors at a meaningful time. This is not done at our convenience or as a routine, but because it's what you know you should do.

3. "Therefore go and make disciples of all nations, baptizing them in the name of the Father and of the Son and the Holy Spirit, and teaching them to obey everything I have commanded you. And surely I am with you always, to the very end of the age" (Matthew 28:19–20).

Okay, now you may be worried about spreading the good news. Don't be. God calls pastors, teachers, sanitation workers, hairdressers, baseball players, businessmen, and businesswomen alike. Spreading the good news doesn't just happen from behind the pulpit, although that's a great place to be. Sharing the good news can be as simple as discovering your general purpose and living joyously every day in response to God's love for you. People will see, and when they ask you why you're different or so joyous, simply tell them the truth. Thus, the good news is spread.

General means relating to or applying to all persons or things. Loving God, loving your neighbor, and telling others the good news is the general purpose for everybody who knows the Lord. Not all will recognize this, but when this truth strikes you, it's kind of like trying on that brand-new baseball glove for the first time. It brings a sense of joy and gratitude that lasts for life.

SPECIFIC PURPOSE

The second type is specific purpose. God made you and formed you with a particular goal for your life. Ephesians 2:10 clearly states this. The purpose God has called you to is *too much* for you to accomplish on your own.

It took living a big chunk of my life to find my specific purpose, but God makes up for time wasted (even though I don't believe any time is "wasted"). He can and will do the same for you as long as you're open to discovering it, if you haven't already done so.

When my specific purpose came into view, it was all I wanted to do. I wanted to stop everything and speak and inspire men to build a Christ-centered legacy. Well, if I would've jumped in blindly, I would've failed to implement God's plan and vision—his way! That's probably why it takes time for many of us to discover our specific purpose.

It's been said that the two most important days in a person's life are the day they're born and the day they find out why. That doesn't mean, however, that the second day is the day it all happens, either instantly or automatically. Spiritual training, prepping, and maturity is a process that must first take place before our specific purpose can realize a maximum harvest.

If you think you know your specific purpose, try the Purpose Test. If you want a jump on discovering it, study your answers to the 5.5 questions and answers.

TOOL #14: THE PURPOSE TEST

If you think you know your specific purpose, put it to the test by asking these questions:

- Does it go against the Scriptures? (see Hebrews 4:12; Psalm 119:105)
- Does this activity bring glory to God? (see 1 Corinthians 10:31)
- Is it profitable to my Christian walk? (see Matthew 16:26)
- Will this build up others? (see 1 Corinthians 14:17)
- Does it take advantage of your gifts or talents? (see Ephesians 2:10)

Now, ask God for answers and be still and listen (see James 1:5–8, Psalm 46:10). Remember, the devil isn't scared of the Jesus *in* you. He's scared when Jesus comes *out* of you.

Don't miss out on, sabotage, or misappropriate your true purpose!

WHAT DOES PURPOSE DO?

I'm sure if you've read with genuine intent, you're feeling a stirring in your belly. Perhaps it feels like excitement, or maybe you sense a bit of nervousness? This stirring is a good thing.

Remember, God wants you to discover your purpose and use it. Here is what you will obtain as you identify more clearly your divine purpose:

- A purpose will motivate you.
- A purpose will keep your priorities straight.
- A purpose will develop your potential.
- A purpose will give you the power to live in the present (and not in the past).
- A purpose will lead you to your destiny.
- A purpose will launch you out of bed.

If the devil can't get your soul, he'll go for your fruitfulness. So be very self-aware and vigilant and value your purpose, because it's a precious gift created especially for you. Finding your identity and purpose is life-changing, but one without the other will still lead to an unfulfilled life. Purposeful identity is the goal.

Now let's look at purposeful identity.

NINE

Purposeful Identity

PURPOSEFUL IDENTITY DEFINED

So what is purposeful identity? It is the process of understanding your true identity and, by doing so, beginning to unlock that specific purpose you were created to do. You see, you can *never* unlock your true purpose without first knowing your true identity. It just can't happen. That's not to say that that you can't be successful; it simply means that what you *were* specifically designed to do can't occur without your addressing the identity question.

Therefore, understanding who you are and why you are is how failure is understood, appreciated, and overcome in life. Let me add one more component, pursuing purposeful passions.

As a Christian, a life coach, and a speaker, I want to see people live fulfilled lives. Knowing your purposeful identity and pursuing your purpose with passion is the only way I see to overcome daunting failure. Plenty of people choose against pursuing their true purpose. Many times this is due to the deception that one direction in life is a "failure-free" offer. Without going after your purpose for being, there is no purposeful identity.

A purposeful identity is more than living a good life. It offers more than any outward appearance or material thing can. Purposeful identity is an internal assurance that you're here for a reason—a specific reason that bears clear witness that you have a God-ordained purpose here on earth. It puts to death the lies spoken over your life, claiming that you are just another person in the crowd and no one special. Or that there are millions just like you, so it doesn't matter if you chase a dream, because someone else who loves to do what you love to do is far better at it than you are, and they will ultimately push you out of the equation. Worse yet, that you're just damaged goods, not even worth God's concern or his interest. All *lies*!

You have a call on your life. No matter the call, no matter how big or small, whatever it is that you are created for, be assured the call is alive. The unchangeable reality of your call is the very reason that you're alive and reading this book. Now is the time to recognize this truth and act on it. Purposeful identity is the revelation of *who* you are, *whose* you are, and *why* you are.

Still feel like you need something more? You do. His name is Jesus. He is the only one who can fulfill our lives and satisfy our innermost longing for identity, purpose, and connection. When I gave my life to Him, I expected angels to come swooping down and lift me high into the air—or better, to be overcome dramatically by His presence and ultimately collapse, overwhelmed with ecstasy. Well, neither experience happened in the way I thought it would. But what did take place was a change in my heart. I knew things were going to be different from that point on.

The same is true for both the revelation of who Jesus Christ is, and for moving into a state of purposeful identity. The fundamental change is felt in our hearts the moment we say yes to Him, but it's only fully manifested after a lifetime of continually walking in that truth.

Below are a few things to remember moving forward with the recognition and discovery of your purposeful identity.

Patience

The Moso bamboo tree is an extraordinary creation that requires much care and even more patience. For successful germination, the seed must be planted to a point of depth where you can't see it. Then it needs water. Water is so critical to the Moso bamboo tree that it must have its share every day. And what's the return?

- Year 1 … nothing visible
- Year 2 … nothing visible
- Year 3 … nothing visible
- Year 4 … nothing visible
- Year 5… explosive growth!

Why?

During the first four years, the root system builds. This root system is strong and wide. Similarly, even though you can't see all the work that's being put in, there is a tremendous amount of preparation going into developing you. This time is necessary to support the great height of the tree and height that God wants you to reach (a maximum harvest).

What do you think your neighbors would say if you watered the same spot, day in and day out, and nothing visibly happened the first four years? They'd probably think you were crazy. But stay patient. There will be plenty of people who try to derail you from your purpose.

Then, during year five, you see the first sprout. It grows rapidly, at roughly three feet per day, to an impressive height of ninety feet. The growth is explosive! The root system was being built behind the scenes to support the coming upward growth. Remember to stay patient.

 "For in this hope we were saved. But hope that is seen is no hope at all. Who hopes for what they already have? But if we hope for what we do not have yet, we wait for it patiently."
— Romans 8:24–25

Perseverance

Every day, you need to water the plant. You can't miss even one day. There will be days when you roll over and look at the clock and will want to skip the watering. It's natural to become tired; you're human. But don't skip it. Value your purpose. There's only one you, and God created you to discover your identity, accomplish your purpose, and live a fulfilled life.

Get up and out there and keep moving forward regardless of how you feel. Like the boxer who gets up at four thirty in the morning to begin his training day with a run while everyone else is asleep, or the musician who plays from early morning to late at night despite the sores on his hand just so he can perfect his gift. The roots being prepared are designed to bring you the vital nutrients needed for strength to stand, and a solid foundation for the days that life tries to shake or uproot you. But you will be well fed and well-grounded, and it will be well worth it.

> *"Not only that, but we also rejoice in our sufferings because we know that suffering produces perseverance; perseverance, character, character, hope. And hope does not disappoint us."*
> — Romans 5:3–5 BSB

> *"Let perseverance finish its work so that you may be mature and complete, not lacking anything."*
> —James 1:4

Humbleness

Be humble. There is power in a purposeful identity. As you discover your giftings, passions, strengths, and brand, you will, by default, grow as a person. The problem with thorn bushes is that they grow rapidly and out of control, spreading to well-kept vegetation and often spoiling the toils of someone else. The Moso bamboo tree grows rapidly but has its direction. There's a difference between this and the thorn bush. Remember, these traits, passions, and identity were given to you as gifts from God. Neither you, I, or anyone else can say that we have earned them. So stay patient, because God reveals them in His timing. Persevere because his timing is coming. And always stay humble because God says:

- I save the humble but bring low those whose eyes are haughty. (Psalm 18:27)
- I guide the humble in what is right and teach them my way. (Psalm 25:9)
- When pride comes, then comes disgrace, but with humility comes wisdom. (Proverbs 11:2)
- I oppose the proud but give grace to the humble. (James 4:6; 1 Peter 5:5)

PULLING IT TOGETHER

God crafted you with a unique identity (who you are) and a specific purpose (why you were created). When you don't take time to work on these areas, you'll experience frustration and unfulfillment.

It's been said that the cemetery is a place where dreams that were never realized, serums that we never discovered, music that was never composed, and books that were never written are buried. This is a crime. Why? Because the world was deprived of these gifts. You see, your gifts maybe yours, but they're not for you to keep to yourself. Your gifts and purpose are *always* designed to bless others, so when you don't act on them, you're actually being selfish. Many would say it is a sin to not do the work to step into the purpose God created you for.

But when you operate fully in your purposeful identity, you experience something that can only be described as pure joy. Remember, life is God's gift to you, and discovering your purposeful identity *and* putting it into action is your gift back to Him.

 "The thief comes only to steal and kill and destroy; I have come that they may have life, and have it to the full."
— John 10:10

Final Thoughts

BELIEVE IN ATTITUDE

Have you ever gone into something expecting one thing, then something completely different plays out? That's the kind of experience I had on May 27, 1995.

The night before, my thoughts ran rampant. One after the other, different scenarios played out in my mind. Each scenario was slightly different, yet I always found myself dwelling on a specific conclusion: that by the end of the next day, my business partner and brother-in-law would have given their lives to Christ.

The night before the Promise Keepers RFK Stadium conference, I carefully thought through all the possible outcomes. By the time the sun gleamed across the horizon, there was little, if anything, that could surprise me. I had it pretty much figured out—or so I thought. Little did I know that it was my life that was about to change forever.

If I were to try to explain what happened that day—my feelings, my thoughts, the purpose I felt, or even how clear my identity was—it would be the equivalent of a newborn baby "telling" his mother that he was hungry for more. My words, or lack thereof, just as the baby, could never be able to explain the experience. The irony here is that many times I've heard guys say things like, "Words just aren't enough to describe ..." or "There isn't a word in the dictionary that could capture ..." Now I know what they meant.

Yet, despite not having adequate words to communicate their thoughts and feelings, their message was never lost. What, then, could meaningfully communicate their experiences if "words aren't enough"? It was their eyes that always told the most impressive piece of the story. A grown man, fearlessly shedding a tear as he told a story about what seems like foolishness to most. That's powerful! When the newborn baby is hungry, she cries out and is heard by her loving mom. It is the child's tearful eyes that cause that mom to stop everything and listen intently. Are my eyes the proof and most convicting part of my own story? If so, I hope you can see teardrops from back on May 27, 1995, spread all through the pages of this book.

That day I crossed the line. I was made new. Up until that time, I thought I was a Christian. But what I thought was wrong, and that day it was as if God took me by the hand and began to show me who I was —a sinner. Little by little he ministered to me, and before I knew it, everything I thought or expected of that day had changed. *I* had changed. Before returning home, I had a new appreciation for my wife, for my kids, for myself, and most importantly for Jesus. It was like scales had leaped off my eyes. I knew change needed to happen, and fast. And by God's grace it did.

Do you want to know what still gets me about that day? I had thought of every possible outcome of our fateful trip, but this was never one of them. Me, a changed man. A man whose chains were broken off. A man whose past could no longer define him. A man who was now a child—a child of the King. But what gets to me about that day is the question, why God would choose me? I wasn't one of the guys walking into the stadium broken or crying—at least I didn't think I was, so why me?

If I can share anything with you—and this is the very reason that I am loyal to Jesus—it's the fact that he loves you. That day I was expecting my business partner and brother-in-law to give their lives to Christ, and they did, but Jesus also called me (among countless others). It was so personal, so perfect, so impossible according to what I thought. You see, I love doing what I do today, which is helping people know the power and ability of Jesus Christ to bring change in their life. Helping these same people find their purposeful identity is what I feel he has entrusted me to do.

Many different actions are taking place as the caterpillar transforms into the butterfly. Actions determine results, and results shape your beliefs. Could a butterfly ever think that all it would ever amount to would be a caterpillar? Of course not! It's already a butterfly—in other words, it has fulfilled its design and purpose. Could a butterfly wish that it were an eagle? Possibly, but why would it?

The world offers many seductions to become something or someone you aren't meant to be. Don't fall for this trap. Don't be "Wrong Way" You, be "Right Road" You. The Identity Thief told the tiny creature that the caterpillar stage was all there was to be experienced. No hope for anything beyond that. We often find ourselves thinking the same way. The truth is that there is something more in you, just waiting to come out. The right attitude opens the door. It's like the first sliver of daybreak shining through the shell of the cocoon. Wider and wider the fragment grows, until one day the cocoon falls away, no longer needed, and those gently crafted wings are ready to fly. Purposeful identity realized!

When the door opens, have faith. Understand that every step won't yield fruit, but with faith, all things are possible. We must learn to trust the one who loves us the most. How different would we act if we knew what God has planned for us? Each person living in the world can discover and live out their purposeful identity. We just need to be available, determined, intentional, and faithful.

Everybody has this potential. The truth is that most people never discover it because they're not only believing lies but also because they have the wrong attitude. They haven't thought about purpose or their identity, let alone a purposeful identity. Instead, they go through life, facing challenges and battles, and they barely scrape by, thinking, *Why me?* What they should be asking is, "For what purposed outcome am I going through this?" Merely asking a different question completely shifts our attitude and changes our perspective. Our attitude then improves significantly; it becomes one that is built on a strong foundation, seeking growth and maturity.

Thank you so much for your time spent reading this book. I sincerely hope your experience has been like my Promise Keepers experience. I hope this book and these 5.5 questions have opened the door to help you be transformed to live out your unique and powerful purposeful identity. I also hope that you now have greater hope than you did when you began your journey with the 5.5 questions.

In addition, my desire is that the words of this book have led you to discover that you have the potential to do whatever it is that you are called to. We just need to make sure that we're asking the right questions, answering them honestly, and then using them to propel us to live out our purposeful identity to fully unlock the God-given potential in us.

One more time:

YOU ARE NOT JUST AN AVERAGE JOE!
YOU WERE BUILT FOR A UNIQUE PURPOSE!

Now go discover it AND live it out!
Again, thank you for reading, and may God bless you!

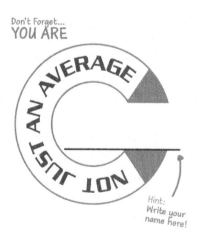

Notes

Introduction

1. "12 Charles Swindoll Quotes from Successories Quote Database." Accessed August 11, 2020. https://www.successories.com/iquote/author/3195/charles-swindoll-quotes/1.

1. Question #1 – What Are Your Strengths?

1. "School Videos - Be like Terry -Fred Fox." The Terry Fox Foundation, September 9, 2019. https://terryfox.org/schoolrun/educators_organizers/schoolvideos/.
2. Marshall, Tabitha, "Terry Fox". In The Canadian Encyclopedia. Historica Canada. Article published May 26, 2008; Last Edited August 05, 2020. https://www.thecanadianencyclopedia.ca/en/article/terry-fox
3. Thomas Ketko | @ThomasKetko April 12, Thomas Ketko, |, Thomas Ketko @ThomasKetko April 12, Dan Robson and Catherine McIntyre, and Gare Joyce. "On 40th Anniversary, Terry Fox's Marathon of Hope Message Is Essential," April 12, 2020. https://www.sportsnet.ca/more/40th-anniversary-terry-foxs-marathon-hope-message-essential/.

3. Question #3 – What Are You Passionate About?

1. "10 Quotes from Billy Graham on the New Year - The Billy Graham Library Blog." The Billy Graham Library, January 13, 2020. https://billygrahamlibrary.org/blog-10-quotes-from-billy-graham-about-the-new-year/.

4. Question #4 – What Is Your Brand?

1. "Harriet Tubman." PBS. Public Broadcasting Service. Accessed August 11, 2020. https://www.pbs.org/wgbh/aia/part4/4p1535.html.
2. Russell, Joyce E. A. "Career Coach: The Power of Using a Name." The Washington Post. WP Company, January 12, 2014. https://www.washingtonpost.com/business/capitalbusiness/career-coach-the-power-of-using-a-name/2014/01/10/8ca03-da0-787e-11e3-8963-b4b654bcc9b2_story.html.
3. Jexi. IMBD. Directed by John Lucas, and Scott Moore. USA, 2019.

5. Question #5 – What Do You Believe?

1. "A Quote by Michelangelo Buonarroti." Goodreads. Goodreads. Accessed August 11, 2020. https://www.goodreads.com/quotes/1191114-the-sculpture-is-already-complete-within-the-marble-block-before.

7. Identity

1. Genius, 2016. https://genius.com/Damian-marley-everybody-wants-to-be-some-body-lyrics.
2. "Stumbling to Success." KristianStill, August 1, 2017. https://www.kristianstill.-co.uk/wordpress/2017/08/01/stumbling-to-success/.

About the Author

Joe Pellegrino is a men's pastor, author, speaker, certified John Maxwell speaker & trainer, consultant and entrepreneur. Joe is the President of Not Just An Average Joe, LLC as well as the President and founder of Legacy Minded Men, whose mission is to "Transform lives by engaging, equipping and encouraging men to build a Christ centered legacy". He has appeared several times on television including Fox News and TBN and been featured on many radio programs, across the country, including Focus on the Family & Family Life Radio, speaking on men's issues. Joe is the co-author of seven books including Safe at Home, Transformed: 7 Pillars of a Legacy Minded Man, That's My Dad!, Fathers Say, The Men's Struggle Cycle, 2 Words From God For The Legacy Minded Man and The Five And A

Half Questions Everyone Must Answer. Joe has also developed and presents several workshops and seminars including Move the Chains, Not Just An Average Joe, The 5.5 Questions Everyone Must Answer and Transformed.

Joe and his wife of 34 years, Bethanne, have three children and one grandchild and reside in Florida. You can reach out to Joe via email at: joe@notjustanaveragejoe.com.

For more information on Joe, including having him speak at your event (live or remote), please visit either:

www.NotJustAnAverageJoe.com
www.LegacyMindedMen.org

Other Books By Joe

Safe at Home
Transformed: 7 Pillars of a Legacy Minded Man
That's My Dad!
Fathers Say
The Men's Struggle Cycle
2 Words from God for the Legacy Minded Man
All books are available through Amazon

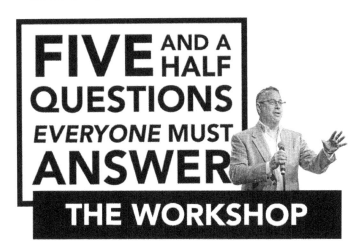

Made in the USA
Monee, IL
02 April 2021

63338722R00085